Praise for the Book

"'Uncaged' delivers a compelling and necessary examination of the youth criminal justice system, centering the lived experiences of Black and marginalized youth. The book immediately draws readers in – placing the most harrowing personal stories at the beginning of each chapter for maximum impact. This approach ensures that the realities of systemic injustice are front and center, setting the stage for a thoughtful blend of narrative and analysis. The author's clear-eyed critique is balanced by actionable recommendations, making 'Uncaged' more than a diagnosis – it's a call for urgent reform. By highlighting both the depth of harm and the pathways to equity, the book challenges readers, advocates, and policymakers to confront uncomfortable truths and work toward a justice system that is truly fair and compassionate. 'Uncaged' is essential reading for anyone committed to real change."

– Tresha Wallace
Nurse/author/Health & Wellness Advocate

"'Uncaged' is a powerful and necessary exposé that confronts the harsh realities still faced by minority youth in Canada's justice system. The stories are raw, pressing, and deeply moving. This book is a call to action and a must-read."

– Hedy Benjamin,
Director of Art

"'Uncaged' is a powerful and thought-provoking book that challenges society's reflex to discipline Black and minority youth through incarceration. It reveals how racialized young people are often misjudged as outsiders and unfairly blamed for struggles that stem from systemic inequities rather than cultural shortcomings. The book highlights how these assumptions fuel punitive responses that prioritize punishment over support when society fails to help young people reach their full potential. By examining public attitudes toward youth crime, 'Uncaged' exposes a disturbing tendency to favour confinement instead of understanding or rehabilitation. It also underscores how racism, poverty, discrimination, and White privilege shape the circumstances of racialized youth while society shifts blame onto them.

The book calls for a reimagined approach to justice, grounded in accountability, community support, dignity, and restoration. 'Uncaged' offers a compelling argument for alternatives that help youth heal, grow, and thrive rather than be locked away."

– Daisy Wright, ACC, CCDP, CCDC,

ICF Associate Certified Coach,

Certified Career Development Practitioner

"I have always understood our Youth Justice System, in particular custody, as an opportunity to support a young person to take new directions in their lives. This opportunity can only be fulfilled through the skill and caring of those working on the frontline directly with the youth. It is the power of relationships that engenders belief, hope, and trust – the fuels for change. 'Uncaged: Freeing Black and Minority Youth from Criminalization' is, in so many ways, a description of the way the Youth Justice system fails to meet this opportunity.

Norma Nicholson delivers a courageous voice from within, describing the harrowing experiences of young people in the system and the moral injury of those working alongside them. A must-read for communities ready to champion change from a system that mirrors racism, struggle, and trauma for Black youth in custody."

– Irwin Elman,
Senior Fellow, Laidlaw Foundation,
President, Defence For Children International Canada

Uncaged

Freeing Black and Minority Youth from Criminalization

Norma Fay Nicholson

Global Book
Publishing

Uncaged
Norma Fay Nicholson

ISBN: 978-1-964644-67-7
Book Design & Publishing done by:
Global Book Publishing
https://globalbookpublishing.com

DISCLAIMER

Readers are encouraged to engage with this content thoughtfully, respecting the perspectives. The author assumes no responsibility or liability for any errors or omissions in this book. It is written from the perspective of the beholder and concerns the experiences of past employees in the youth justice system.

The intention is to shed light on important issues surrounding the youth justice system and foster understanding and dialogue. Should anyone recognize a role that they may have participated in, note that the characters bear no relation to the living persons.

It is essential to be aware that the stories, anecdotes, and discussions in this publication are based on real-life experiences and may evoke strong emotions. Reader discretion is advised, especially for individuals with personal connections to this system and for those whose emotions may be affected by the subject matter.

I aim to create a respectful and empathetic space for these narratives while acknowledging the complexities of the topics discussed. Please be reminded to approach these contents with sensitivity and an open mind.

> *The role of a writer is not to say what we all can say, but what we are unable to say.*
>
> ***–Anaïs Nin***

All featured images are by Hedy Benjamin, and the author has the artist's permission to use them.

Change will not come if we wait for some other person or some other time. We are the ones we've been waiting for. We are the change that we seek.

– Barack Obama, Former (and first African-American) President of the USA

Keep exploring. Keep dreaming. Keep asking why. Don't settle for what you already know.

– Barack Obama

Don't bring the negative to my door.

– Maya Angelou, Activist and Author

Darkness cannot drive out darkness; only light can do that.

– Martin Luther King, Jr., American Minister and Activist

You have been taught to be second-class; you are not born that way.

– Lena Horne, Black Activist

Education is the most powerful weapon you can use to change the world.

– Nelson Mandela, Activist and former President of South Africa

This book is dedicated to Black and minority youths who have their future negatively impacted by the systems and institutions that oppress them.

Table of Contents

Preface

Not everything that is faced can be changed. But nothing can be changed until it is faced.

– James Baldwin

This book places no blame on individuals for the horrific situations that have impacted the lives of Black and other minority youths while they were incarcerated. Some Youth Service Officers have acted professionally, treated Black and minority youths with care, and given them hope for their futures. Those men and women who have devoted their careers to building a better world for others sometimes suffer retribution from their colleagues who disapprove of helping these youth. Some, beaten down by the retribution and can't bear it any longer, sadly leave their positions.

Others have used brutality and power to shame, belittle, punish, and demean the youths who were placed in their care. It did not matter whether that youth was in detention for immigration purposes, awaiting trial when they were supposed to be considered innocent until proven guilty, or was sentenced to serve time in custody.

The author uses a health equity lens to explore the issues and explain why they should be changed. When delivering healthcare to youths in custody, healthcare providers do not need to discuss the crime that led to their custody. While receiving healthcare, however, the youths may share with the professional delivering the care, to their knowledge, why they were arrested. Through healthcare delivery, it becomes clear why the youths end up in the justice system.

When one recalls the teenage years, it is clear how often teens would not readily inform parents that they couldn't see or hear properly, they had unprotected sex and now have a sexually transmitted infection which has been intentionally shared, an inability to read or write, taking drugs or alcohol, and have been involved with gang activities.

Therefore, these ordinary and genuine developmental issues shouldn't lead to criminalization, mistreatment, or incarceration of our youths. This book examines how systemic inequities and racism, masked as discipline and justice, have damaged young lives and how equitable healthcare can reveal pathways for reformation.

Purpose

Change will not come if we wait for some other person or some other time. We are the ones we've been waiting for; we are the change that we will seek.

– Barack Obama

The book aims to serve the following purposes in the pages ahead:

- Deliver education that provides information on how prevalent it is in our society to criminalize Black and minority male youth.
- Assist parents in learning about the justice system and ways to keep their children in the community, helping them reach their potential.
- Provide an opportunity to highlight the contents of the Youth Criminal Justice Act in layperson's terms. The act explains the law governing the management of delinquent behaviour among youths who come into contact with the criminal justice system.
- Examine some of the factors that lead to the over-incarceration of Black and minority male youth.
- The texts share some of the author's lived experiences as a healthcare leader at a secure youth custody facility.

- Engage in and explore ways for systemic changes.
- Challenge the perceptions and assumptions about the delinquent behaviours of adolescents.
- Explain why the author does not support the use of incarceration for managing delinquent behaviours, as this has been proven to be a total failure.
- Share alternatives to incarceration that have been researched and used by organizations in Canada and other parts of the world.
- Share strategies on how the various entangled systems could work together better and more effectively.
- Encourage the reader to actively participate as a cog in the wheel of change rather than remain complicit.

Introduction

> *Even though news stories about youth and crime shake our sense of safety, the facts do not always support this dangerous and fictitious narrative. When our children and teens get in trouble, we know they need support, not incarceration.*
>
> ***– Josh Rovner, The Sentencing Project, 2023***

When recognizing systemic challenges within the Canadian youth criminal justice system, it is important to acknowledge the historical and present-day impacts of colonialism and systemic discrimination, which include but are not limited to the over-representation of Black people throughout the criminal justice system. This over-incarceration exacerbates pre-existing structural barriers rooted in systemic racism. The intersection of racial disparities and the justice system involvement creates many obstacles for Black people to advance in our society. It begins in childhood and persists into adulthood.

Do you know that, as a society, we could all amplify the voices of Black youths in our communities? Do you celebrate them through their boundless potential, creativity, and inspiring voices that will shape our future? Do you trust them to be agents of change? If you answered yes, why would you support the incarceration of Black and minority youth?

There are overwhelming statistics that demonstrate that incarceration is a failed approach to use when young Black/minority males encounter the justice system. Punitive approaches are failing young people, their families, and the community. We must prioritize health and well-being. What should we do if we do not incarcerate them when their challenging behaviours cannot be managed in the community? As the author, I will delve into dynamic alternatives to incarceration that foster healthier, safer communities.

It has been thirteen years since I retired from leading a healthcare team at Ontario's largest secure youth custody facility. I spent the last five years of my nursing career working with an energetic, strong team focused on youth health and well-being. I was slowly pushed out the door of the organization by the administration team because my core values of wanting rehabilitation for Black and minority youths did not align with theirs. They focused on punishment, while my team wanted health and well-being.

I sit at my desk at home and reflect that my nightmares have become fewer. I go to sleep each night soundly and do not wake up to go to work, seeing and hearing the agony of Black males and other minority youths in custody being abused physically, emotionally, or psychologically. Though traumatized, I left with my integrity, self-esteem, and sanity.

You may ask me why I waited so long to share those experiences. As a Black person seeing the atrocities, I needed time to heal, self-align, and be stronger to document these lived experiences. My subconscious has released me from these nightmares as I tell myself that sharing some of these horrific situations with the world will not only release me from the vicarious trauma I experienced, including recurring thoughts and flashbacks, but will also help with the required changes. I am taking constructive actions in assisting communities, parents, governments, and society to understand that there needs to be an ideological shift about the purpose of the incarceration of children and youth.

Having concrete lived experiences makes the harsh realities of some incarcerated youths more real. There should be no incarceration for this age group. Incarceration is a failed attempt to manage the challenging behaviours that lead to the crimes committed by young Black males. There are better ways to achieve public safety. Though I authored two previous books, *Young Lives on the Line: You Can Make a Difference* and *Walking Miles in Sensible Shoes: A Nurse Looks Back at her Vocation,* I refrained at that time from writing about the lived experiences of leading a healthcare team in a secure youth custody facility. I needed to heal from the trauma, and this takes time with the help of a professional.

In this book, I will provide many examples of what should be done in collaboration with various systems and community partners to keep our children in our communities and help them reach their potential. I will share examples of what happens to a few of the male youths during their incarceration and why there is deterioration and deficiency in our society in managing youth crimes. I want to be a small part of that "cog in the wheel of change" in my lifetime.

As you walk around the grounds of this youth custody facility, don't be fooled by the façade of a university campus and adjacent mid-size dormitories. The 9-foot chain-linked fence merely gives you a glimpse of the hellish life inside. I was on my way to the facility's school, accompanied by two youth services officers and five youths who were on their way to school.

One youth asks the other, "Are you sure you want to go to school today after all that shit happened at breakfast?"

The youth responded, "We are made more into criminals when we are here."

The two youth service officers remembered the response and followed up after school to demand an explanation from the youths. The subsequent questioning of the youth asked him to demonstrate how he had become the worst criminal, and he refused, which was a reprimand in and of itself. It was uncalled for and set a precedent in silencing him and other youth from voicing their concerns or coming forward to effect change. The next day, he was never seen at that facility, as he had been transferred out because he was now labelled a troublemaker.

Come along with me on this journey to understand what must be done before our Black and minority youths get involved with the criminal justice system and why other youths with similar backgrounds do not follow that path. Why do Black and other minority youths remain on the margins of our community's well-being? Why do even their families and society stigmatize and marginalize them? Why do we see more Black and minority youths in the "System?" Why are White children who commit similar crimes not incarcerated?

We are seeing a social crisis in which there is an undeniable influx of youths into the criminal justice system. Sadly, even though all racial groups are committing crimes, those who are detained in provincial jails are disproportionately Black and minorities from low socio-economic backgrounds.

What must a community and family do to ensure these youths reach their potential? How do we keep them in our communities, living very productive and healthy lives? We must look at the importance of education, racism, mental illness, addictions, and why Black students are not given the resources to reach their potential. To meet the challenges and opportunities for change, let's also look at why our government and society support the incarceration of young persons. What changes are needed to understand that this is not the solution to keep communities safe from crimes? The research tells us about the adverse effects of incarceration and what should be done differently. We must work together to end imprisonment for a better society for all. I will share some dynamic changes we can make together to enhance the lives of all youths and their families.

CHAPTER 1

Broken Systems, Breaking Youths

Breaking News That Could Be True

Imagine, for a moment, that you are listening to the local news and hear the "Breaking News." The pathways for changes in the youth justice system, aligned with the Youth Criminal Justice Act, have passed the third reading in our Canadian Parliament. After five years of trial and error, advocates have succeeded in ending the incarceration of Black and minority youth.

- All youths between 12 and 17 will no longer be incarcerated for more than 72 hours until specific resources are found in their communities to meet the needs that are identified by the youth justice system.
- All youths who present with delinquent behaviours will be redirected to established community diversion/treatment/rehabilitation programs to meet their individual needs within this timeframe.
- Community resources will be available to meet the needs of families and their children.
- Additional diversion and restorative programs are being added, with training for multiple professionals.

- Parents and guardians are encouraged to attend educational sessions and connect with care communities.
- All youth jails will be closed within three years and refurbished as Community Youth Hubs.

This is vastly different from the norm and feels like a dream come true. Even with the legislated law, the Youth Criminal Justice Act, many youths of colour are languishing in jail, especially in Canada and the United States. Some are detained, awaiting their day in court, while others are serving their sentences.

Would you like to change a youth's life forever? What can you do to significantly positively impact the lives of Black and minority youths before and after they become involved in the youth criminal justice system?

As a healthcare leader at a large, secure youth custody facility in Ontario, I am expected to work 8–10 hours daily and be on call 24 hours. I drove in through the blinding snowfall at 7 a.m. on a freezing-cold Tuesday. I picked up my cell and called my husband at a red traffic light at one of the main intersections.

I said, "Hon, I'm so sorry to wake you again, but I need you to pray for my safety because the weather is so bad; many vehicles are sliding in the snow."

He said, "Continue slowly; I will be praying, and call me when you arrive in the parking lot at work."

Within 40 minutes of speaking with my husband, I drove into the parking lot at work. I prayed all the way, and knowing he was doing the same kept me going. I called him and said, "I have arrived safely."

He said, "Really try to have a good day. I hope that the roads are cleared of snow on your way home."

Despite travel challenges, I arrived at work at 8 a.m. Now, walk with me as I pick up and log out my department's keys at the security desk. For precautionary reasons, the healthcare department is accessible only with a safety key. I could hear loud, unintelligible voices when I inserted the department's key into the lock.

When I opened the department's door, I was surprised to see five individuals from other departments having a heated conversation. The dreaded silence occurred as they saw me. I said good morning to all, then opened my office, took off my coat, and laid my handbag and coat on the chair. Within a few seconds, I was swarmed by these five individuals inside my office. Instead of acknowledging them, I asked for the department's nurse and, in the same breath, why they were all there.

Saved by Rose, the RN who came through the door to the department.

She asked, "Why are all these folks in your office?"

There were two facility managers, two front-line security staff, and a deputy administrator. Almost simultaneously, they responded, "We need to tell you what happened overnight and ask if you would go to the hospital to see James, a youth from Cottage Five."

Indeed, it is a very unusual request! I invited all of them to sit at the department's large table. I want to hear from the nurse first; what did she observe when she came on duty at 6 a.m.?

The Horrifying Story

James is being held in detention while he waits for his court date. He has been waiting for this date for eight weeks because his single mom lives in poverty and is unable to pay for bail or know of anyone who could post bail for him. It has been rumoured that the police know him. He is also known as the pill-popper who takes many prescription pills when he is depressed. A few years ago, he wanted to die by suicide in the community, but was prevented by his older brother. Being in jail does nothing good for his chronic medical issues; they will be with him for his lifetime.

He has "Sickle Cell Disease," and this diagnosis is known by all who interact with him daily. Each youth services officer was given informed education about James's diagnosis due to the negative impact that certain activities could have on his body. In addition, there was written information to guide what they do when he complained of having pain. In some simple situations where he may be placed, such as walking outside in the snow or rain, he could have sickling of his red blood cells. It blocks the flow of blood to all the organs in his body and causes excruciating pain, especially in his joints.

Along with receiving scheduled medications during the day, James was assessed every evening when the medication nurse made her last round just before his bedtime. She left written instructions and two doses of pain medication with the youth services officer to be given to him 4 hours apart should he request this medication. Note that these tablets are not narcotics, as it would be illegal to leave such medication with a youth service officer. The care plan, developed with input from James, the healthcare team professionals, youth service officers, and managers, directed everyone who saw James during the night to discuss any issues regarding his pain control with the "on-call manager." All youth service officers were provided with health education about Sickle Cell disease. Still, not all wanted to give over-the-counter medication to the youth, stating that *we are not nurses*. An information sheet was left at the desk to assist everyone on duty in deciding when he would receive his medication. They had the green light to call the on-call manager for decision-making or to administer the medication.

The Nurse Shared What James Reported

About 3 hours after the evening nurse gave him two tablets of his medication, he told the officer that his pain was getting worse. The officer responded, "You have just received medication." By this time, the nurse had gone off duty, and additional information was also left in the main office for the on-call facility manager. James reported that he stayed awake due to the excruciating pain he was experiencing.

As the pain worsened, he cried out for help and was met with responses such as, "You baby, go to sleep. If you are such a baby, why the hell are you in jail? You should be sticking to your momma." He was not given any medication to control his pain overnight.

The following morning, the nurse arrived by 6 a.m. to assess James's status. The youth service officer accompanied the nurse to enter his cell. He reported that he gave up asking for pain medication most of the night because, from the responses of the youth service officers, he knew that he would not receive any. He had lain on the bed and tried to fold himself into a ball, which seemed to lower his pain slightly.

He was seen to be perspiring and shaking, and his voice was almost inaudible. The nurse knew right then that he was in a Sickle Cell Crisis and requested that the manager for that cell block be called and that an ambulance be ordered as soon as possible to take James to the hospital. She then informed her nursing colleague, who was visiting the other areas, to assess all other youth, as she needed to stay with him. She asked that the on-call senior manager be informed about the youth's medical situation. She also asked her colleague to prepare an oxygen setup for James and bring it to his cell. She gave him two tablets of his pain medication and sips of water, but he was unable to swallow the pills. He said he could not sit up, so the nurse kneeled by his side to help him drink some water. He was then placed on low-flow oxygen via nasal prongs.

According to nursing standards of practice, an RN can give this form of oxygen while waiting to transfer a youth to the hospital. An in-charge nurse would inform the physician upon his arrival in the department within the next 2 hours that the youth had become ill and was sent to the hospital.

The ambulance arrived soon, and the paramedics conducted a further assessment and started an intravenous line to give James much-needed fluids and added medication. He was then transported to the hospital, accompanied by two youth service officers and the paramedics. He was assessed and admitted to the Intensive Care Unit (ICU).

When the nurse completed her report, one of the facility's managers responded, "That is not how all this happened."

I listened, not wanting to get into a conflict. I thanked the nurse and asked her to check on her colleague; we would have a short meeting within a few minutes.

I gave the manager a copy of the nursing report and respectfully requested that all those present meet to discuss what had occurred on the night shift, and we could meet later in the morning. I also reminded them that the young person had been admitted to the hospital and that I didn't need to go, as they had requested. When I later met with the two nurses, we called the ICU manager at the hospital, who gave an update on James' status.

We debriefed on the situation and identified potential gaps in support for the youth services officers and the custodial youth. I thanked the nurses for managing the youth's care professionally. The original nursing document was filed on the youth's chart, and a copy was forwarded to our healthcare deputy.

Many in-depth treatments were administered in the hospital to save James' life. When anyone goes into a Sickle Cell crisis and is deprived of medication to control pain to enable the sickled red cells to work, it takes over 72 hours or more before that person is stable. He stayed in the hospital for two months.

During his stay in the hospital, a representative from the senior management team in the facility, representatives from the hospital, and his mother, along with the help of a legal aid lawyer, petitioned the youth justice system and asked that he be sent on house arrest until his trial.

A reminder that the healthcare team does not get involved with the reason for incarceration unless they are asked to assist with discharge planning. Their role is to deliver specific healthcare servicces to help incarcerated youths achieve adequate health and function more effectively. The healthcare team had no further involvement in the youth's care, nor did the administrator or the facility manager request a follow-up meeting.

So, your question as the observer may be: *Why is this teen being kept in jail when he has a debilitating medical disease?*

Why would Youth Services Officers, who are trained to support an incarcerated youth with rehabilitation around their developmental stages, treat a young person so disdainfully?

My response is that the system does not work in favour of Black teens. They are often viewed as criminals and drug addicts who have no second chances; they are known to the police; this is also double jeopardy; there are no planned diversion plans for them as directed by the YCJA. Being known to the police could be as simple as being stopped and asked, "Where are you going at this time?" It is documented in the officer's notes as an encounter with a Black youth.

Black families must educate themselves about the best way to talk to their children about racism and prepare them for racist encounters, whether or not they are incarcerated.

A Bit about Sickle Cell Disease

1. Sickle cell disease is a group of inherited disorders affecting red blood cells. A child develops sickle cell disease when they receive two sickle genes, one from each parent. Sickle cell disease is found among Blacks and other nationalities, such as the Portuguese.
2. It affects red blood cells, which are usually round, causing them to change into a C shape and become stiff and distorted. These sickled cells have difficulty passing through blood vessels, causing tissue damage, and they are

rapidly destroyed. They obstruct blood flow throughout the body, causing a range of ailments.

3. These ailments include fatigue, excessive pain, anemia, pale skin, pale nails and tongue, and a White bottom of the feet. Red cell breakdown produces bilirubin, which causes "Jaundice," in which the whites of the eyes appear yellow.
4. The pain and swelling are caused by sickled cells damaging the bone marrow (a painful crisis). Most pains are worse when the weather is cold and wet. Common causes of pain include cold, damp environments and even cold showers!
5. In older children (teens) and adults, the pain affects the bones close to the joints.
6. It causes sores on the legs and damage around the ankles (a joint), leading to leg ulcers that must be treated quickly to prevent amputation of the leg.
7. People with sickle disease are more likely to have serious infections, grow more slowly, get sudden and severe anemia, and develop pneumonia and strokes. These children can die quickly if not given the required health and emotional support.

One is not even required to know the Youth Criminal Justice Act legislation, which clearly states that children must be treated as children, not adults. In this circumstance, he needs only to be treated as a human being. Several measures can be taken to prevent or effectively treat these complications. Every possible means must be used to help individuals with this disease achieve a pain-free status. A slight stomach-ache can trigger a crisis. Even if your perspective is that they are drug-seeking, not treating the pain will shorten lives.

Changes take time, and for the Black and minority youths who are incarcerated, that change is urgent. Sadly, two racialized youth service officers who interacted with him traumatized him almost to his death. This youth told the hospital staff that he had silently said goodbye to his mother because he felt that his death was imminent. There is presently no zero tolerance for measuring officers' transgressions. The senior staff, administration, and youth service officers are trained in effective strategies to work with Black and minority youth, but most focus on punishment instead of rehabilitation.

Some are very culturally insensitive and forget their cultural background to fit into a mould. They pretend not to know how their racist remarks and practices alienate and oppress Black youths who do not benefit from any rehabilitation while incarcerated. On their release, they are thrown back into the community with significant behavioural problems worse than when they entered youth custody. Being often subject to unnecessary punitive measures, dehumanization, neglect, brutality, and harassment, they are broken and re-traumatized on release. One can only imagine experiencing horrific pain for over 7 hours and being ignored. This stores up many negative emotions, such as anger and rage.

The Youth Criminal Justice Act exists because research on children's and youth's developmental stages and data collection indicate that they are not little adults and should be treated as such in all situations. There are a large number of alternative processes and programs that can be used to prevent a young person from being incarcerated. Many are psychologically broken when they are discharged from incarceration in the youth criminal justice system.

CHAPTER 2

Rights, Reform, & Reality

The Youth Criminal Justice Act (YCJA)

The Youth Criminal Justice Act (YCJA) is the official work of the Government of Canada. Permission is given to reproduce and use accurately. The Act appears here as documented on Canada's Youth Justice Website.

The Youth Criminal Justice Act Summary and Background[1]

The *Youth Criminal Justice Act* is the law that governs Canada's youth justice system. It applies to youths aged 12–17 who are alleged to have committed criminal offences. In over a century of youth justice legislation in Canada, there have been three youth justice statutes: the *Juvenile Delinquents Act* (1908–1984), the *Young Offenders Act* (YOA) (1984–2003), and the *Youth Criminal Justice Act* (YCJA, 2003 to present). A set of amendments to the YCJA was adopted by Parliament in 2012. The purpose of this document is to

[1] https://www.justice.gc.ca/eng/rp-pr/cj-jp/yj-jj/pdf/back-hist.pdf

explain the background of the YCJA, to provide a summary of its main provisions and the rationale behind them, and to highlight the experience under the YCJA.

Background

On April 1, 2003, the YCJA came into force, completely replacing the previous legislation, the YOA. The YCJA introduced significant reforms to address concerns about how the youth justice system had evolved under the YOA. These concerns included the overuse of the courts and incarceration in less-severe cases, disparity and unfairness in sentencing, a lack of effective reintegration of young people released from custody, and the need to consider the interests of victims better. The YCJA provided the legislative framework for a fairer and more effective youth justice system. The amendments adopted by Parliament in 2012 aimed to strengthen the youth justice system's response to repeat and violent offenders.

Preamble and Declaration of Principles

The YCJA contains a Preamble and a Declaration of Principles that apply throughout the Act. The Preamble contains significant statements from Parliament about the values upon which the legislation is based. These statements can be used to help interpret the legislation and include the following:

- Society is responsible for addressing the developmental challenges and needs of young persons.
- Communities and families should work in partnership with others to prevent youth crime by addressing its underlying causes, responding to young people's needs, and providing guidance and support.

- Accurate information about youth crime, the youth justice system, and effective measures should be publicly available.
- Young persons have special guarantees of their rights and freedoms, including those set out in the United Nations Convention on the Rights of the Child.
- The youth justice system should consider victims' interests and ensure accountability through meaningful consequences, rehabilitation, and reintegration.
- The youth justice system should reserve its most serious interventions for the most serious crimes and reduce the over-reliance on incarceration.

The Declaration of Principles sets out the legislative policy framework. Unlike previous youth justice legislation, the YCJA guides the priority that is to be given to key principles.

The Declaration of Principles provides that:

- The youth justice system is intended to protect the public by (i) holding young persons accountable through measures that are proportionate to the seriousness of the offence and the degree of responsibility of the young person, (ii) promoting the rehabilitation and reintegration of young persons, and (iii) supporting crime prevention by referring young persons to programs or agencies in the community to address the circumstances underlying their offending behaviour.
- The youth justice system must be separate from the adult system and must be based on the principle of diminished moral blameworthiness or culpability.

- The youth justice system must reflect the fact that young people lack the maturity of adults. The youth system differs from the adult system in many respects: accountability measures are consistent with the young persons' lower level of maturity, procedural protections are enhanced, rehabilitation and reintegration are given special emphasis, and the importance of timely intervention is recognized.
- Young persons are to be held accountable through interventions that are fair and in proportion to the seriousness of the offence.
- Within the limits of fair and proportionate accountability, interventions should reinforce respect for societal values, encourage the repair of harm done, be meaningful to the young person, respect gender, ethnic, cultural, and linguistic differences, and respond to the needs of Aboriginal young persons and young persons with special requirements.
- Youth justice proceedings require a recognition that young persons have rights and freedoms and special guarantees of these rights and freedoms; courtesy, compassion, and respect for victims; the opportunity for victims to be informed and to participate; and that parents be informed and encouraged to participate in addressing the young person's offending behaviour.

In addition to the Preamble and the Declaration of Principles, the YCJA includes other, more specific principles to guide decision-making at key points in the youth justice process: Extrajudicial

Measures, Youth Sentencing, and Custody and Supervision. These additional principles are discussed below.

Extrajudicial Measures

Background: Experience in Canada and other countries shows that measures outside the court process can effectively respond to less serious youth crime. One of the key objectives of the YCJA is to increase the use of effective and timely non-court responses to less serious offences by youth. These extrajudicial measures provide meaningful consequences, such as requiring the young person to repair the harm done to the victim. They also enable early intervention with young people and offer the broader community the opportunity to play an important role in developing community-based responses to youth crime. Increasing the use of non-court responses also enables the courts to focus on the more serious cases of youth crime.

Before the YCJA, youth courts dealt with many minor offences that did not require a court proceeding to hold the young person accountable adequately. In addition, the extent to which cases were diverted from the court process varied considerably between provinces.

YCJA Provisions: The YCJA contains provisions to increase the appropriate use of extrajudicial measures for less serious offences, including the following principles:

- Extrajudicial measures should be used in all cases where they would be adequate to hold the young person accountable.
- Extrajudicial measures are presumed to be adequate to hold first-time, non-violent offenders accountable.

- Extrajudicial measures may be used if the young person has previously dealt with them or has been found guilty of an offence. As amended in 2012, the YCJA requires police to keep records of any extrajudicial measures used with a young person. These records will better inform the police so they can take appropriate action regarding subsequent alleged offences.

The YCJA also sets out clear objectives to guide the use of extrajudicial measures, including repairing the harm caused to the victim and the community, providing an opportunity for victims to participate in decisions, ensuring that the measures are proportionate to the seriousness of the offence, and encouraging the involvement of families, victims, and other members of the community.

The YCJA requires police officers to consider the use of extrajudicial measures before deciding to charge a young person. Police and prosecutors are specifically authorized to use various types of extrajudicial measures:

- *Taking no further action.*
- *Warnings*, which are informal warnings by police officers.
- *Police cautions*, which are more formal warnings by the police. The YCJA authorizes provinces to establish police cautioning programs. Police cautions may take the form of a letter to the young person and their parents, or involve a process in which the young person and their parents are requested to appear at a police station to speak with a senior police officer.

- *Crown cautions* are like police cautions, but prosecutors issue them after the police refer the case to them. In one province where they are currently being used, Crown cautions are in the form of letters to the young person and the parents.
- *Referrals,* which are referrals by police officers of young persons to community programs or agencies that may help them avoid committing offences. The referral may be to various community resources, including recreation programs and counselling agencies.
- *Extrajudicial sanctions*, which are the most formal type of extrajudicial measure, may be pre-charge or post-charge. Unlike other types of extrajudicial measures, they may be used only if the young person admits responsibility for the offending behaviour and consents to the sanction. The admission of responsibility is not a guilty plea to the alleged offence. Before consenting, the young person must be informed of the sanction and allowed to consult with a lawyer. The province's Attorney General must determine that there is sufficient evidence to proceed with a prosecution of the offence. In addition, the sanctions must be part of an extrajudicial sanctions program designated by the Attorney General. If the young person fails to comply with the terms and conditions of the sanction, the case may proceed through the court process. An extrajudicial sanction can be used only if a warning, caution, or referral cannot adequately address the young person's behaviour.

– Originally published on February 19, 2002;
Youth Criminal Justice Act (SC 2002, c.)

The Youth Criminal Justice Act in Layman's Terms

The Youth Criminal Justice Act governs Canada's youth justice system and provides community alternatives for youths who get in trouble with the law. This law came into force in April 2003. The new legislation introduced significant changes to address concerns in the youth criminal justice system and reduce the use of jail time for youths. It is an educational tool that explains why adolescents engage in delinquent behaviour and offers alternatives to address these issues. This Act applies to all youth; however, it does not always apply to Black and minority youth, depending on who administers justice.

From the inception of the Youth Criminal Justice Act, youth justice has been an evolving system seeking effective strategies to reduce recidivism and re-offending. Changes are required from the past management of youths in the youth criminal justice system.

Why is there a need to better understand and apply this Act? Knowing the Act will ensure that youths are provided with community alternatives to jail. Practitioners and program developers will be able to support positive outcomes for youths involved with the law. The Act emphasizes rehabilitation, providing the youths with the opportunity to learn from mistakes, accept consequences, and make amends while in the community. The media will also gain in-depth knowledge of why a youth who commits a crime should not be identified. Daily, the media requests that police services release the name of a youth who has been arrested. These requests contradict the legislation's directives, which require protection for young persons who become involved in the justice system. One measure is not to identify them in the media, ensuring that, once rehabilitation occurs, they have opportunities to reach their full potential.

Racial discrimination is one of the reasons why Black and minority youths are seen in some aspects of society as having low potential, prone to criminality, and as being older than they are. They are over-represented in the youth criminal justice system, and many people blame them and their families for this negative outcome. These negative perceptions and assumptions held by many override the full application of the Act.

Research has shown that this over-representation of incarcerated Black youths is often due to the negative ways they are evaluated in our broader society and in the systems that oppress them, such as Policing, Children's Aid Societies, Schools, and the Justice System.

Many adults need to remember the behaviour they displayed as teenagers. They often deny their past delinquent behaviours or say they were good boys and girls who did not get into trouble. Other individuals say the YCJA is soft on crimes that youths commit, and they should be punished rather than allowed rehabilitation. Some folks are clearly racist because it is assumed that primarily Black youths carry out criminal acts.

Did you know that before YCJA came into force, the youths awaiting their trials were kept in the same facilities as adult inmates? Moreover, page 7 of the YCJA addresses the overuse of detaining youths in jail before their court trial. An alarming number of youths were detained for minor offences in the same areas as adults to meet their "social welfare" needs (as a substitute for child protection, mental and other social measures). It is quite frightening to think about some of the horrific incidents documented in that mix.

The Criminal Code of Canada is a federal law that governs Canada's adult justice system and can be applied to young persons aged 18 years and older. This Code mentions some offences that apply to youths but are prosecuted under the procedures set out in the youth justice legislation. Where young persons are mentioned in the YCJA, this refers to a person aged 12 but less than 18 years old. The YJCA focuses on increasing the use of **effective, timely measures outside the court process** for less serious youth crimes. Police services and prosecutors are authorized to use various measures outside the court to hold youths accountable without proceeding through the formal process.

Some of these measures include taking no further action, issuing a warning, a police caution, a crown caution, or referring the young person to a community program or agency designed to help them change their behaviour. These measures provide meaningful consequences that allow the young person to repair the harm done to the victim. They also offer opportunities for communities to develop community-based responses to youth crime. The judge has a range of alternative measures to choose from that can be used to hold the young person accountable without proceeding through the formal court process.

Diverting youths from youth court involvement, reducing the length of incarceration, and increasing community involvement, such as rehabilitative programs, should be a central focus in efforts to reduce racial and ethnic disparities and improve the outcomes in our country's youth justice systems.

Moving young people away from the criminal justice system and offering alternatives are much better ways to ensure community safety. Research has shown that relying on tools of arrest, prosecution, and incarceration has not made us safer and harms our communities. There is this racial divide, particularly among Black communities and communities of colour, as it is a fact that there is an over-incarceration of Black youths not only in Canada but also in the United States.

Several provisions in the Youth Criminal Justice Act provide special considerations to prevent young persons from being incarcerated. The criminal justice system for youths is very separate from that of adults. The focus must be on rehabilitation and reintegration, as well as enhanced protection, to ensure they are treated fairly and that their rights, including privacy rights, are protected. Rather than charging youths for a minor offence that takes up much time in the courts, they could be required to complete the alternative measures noted in the Act, holding them responsible for their actions more quickly and effectively.

Built into the Diversion programs are ways to reinforce respect for societal values, encourage the repair of harm done to the victim and the community, and hold young people accountable for their offending behaviour. Parents/guardians should be informed of the measures or proceedings involving their children and encouraged to support them in addressing their offending behaviours. Remember that each youth has different circumstances that need to be addressed.

Your Goal as Black Parents/Guardians and Community

1. Love your children, listen to them, believe what they tell you until proven otherwise, give them a voice to speak the truth, and build incredible trust and effective relationships with them.
2. Talk to your children about racism to prepare them for encounters and give them the tools they will need to survive and thrive in the face of racism. Teach them to ask questions respectfully while managing their emotions.
3. Raise strong Black children by learning about their developmental stages and the specific information they need, especially as they transition through adolescence.
4. Remember that children's and youths' brains continue to develop, even up to age 25, to fully understand negative behaviours and their consequences.
5. Learn as much as you can about systemic racism and use the tools you gain to interact effectively.
6. Learn ways to intervene and prevent your children from engaging in criminal activity. Teach them that it is okay to say NO to things that could lead them into delinquent behaviour.
7. Teach them life skills such as making effective decisions, managing conflicts, and staying safe on social media.
8. Ask for help clarifying unclear situations. Many online resources, books, and pamphlets are available; some can be found in your community libraries.

9. Teach your children to know their rights when they encounter police who are asking them questions.
10. Learn that even when a Black or minority youth does not become involved in the criminal justice system, you must acquire knowledge about the opportunities for diversion.
11. Lead with love and be willing to learn and also relearn.
12. Be reminded that implicit biases extend to young people's families of colour, where court officials often assess them more harshly than White families. These negative assessments limit diversion opportunities. Many people are unaware of normal adolescent behaviours.
13. Research has shown that many Black families do not seek professional help for mental illness for themselves or their children due to the heightened stigma, shame, and expectations that they should always be strong. Learn the signs and symptoms of mental well-being so that when you or your child experiences a change, you can seek help from a family doctor or the Kids Helpline, available in every state.

Remember that discrimination can affect how the world relates to you and your family, and how you relate to the world. Education helps to equalize most of these factors. Black families must have access to information and to culturally relevant and responsive programs and services when needed to address their families' needs.

Despite the resilience of Black families and the capacity and strength of Black parents, research indicates that Black parents, children, and youths grapple with multiple intersectional issues. These issues range from poor mental health to poor educational outcomes in the Canadian public school system and disproportionate numbers of children in the Child Welfare System. Sadly, the adverse treatment they receive is one of the reasons they become involved in delinquent behaviours.

Changed Since YCJA Took Effect in 2003

Below are some key points that have changed since the Youth Criminal Justice Act came into force in 2003:

1. Some rehabilitative custody and supervision programs in communities have been receiving short-term funding from provinces to enhance treatment for seriously marginalized and high-need youths. This approach requires long-term financing to sustain them and to measure outcomes.
2. The legislative framework for youth justice and the mandatory consideration of eliminating societal views that treat some youths as *little adults* have made the system take it seriously, where children are no longer jailed with adults or being tried in adult courts. (Recently, in Ontario, a large courthouse was built in Toronto, and unfortunately, both adults and children can be found in the same setting.)
3. The media and specific aspects of society continue to press for in-depth information about youths who face criminal charges and request changes to the Youth Criminal Justice Act (YCJA). Many people continue to believe that punishment is more effective than treatment and rehabilitation.

4. There are instances where the mental health of the youths is not being addressed and taken seriously by looking at the root causes of the behaviours.
5. The use of custody is slightly reduced as it is no longer the go-to solution and is reserved for the most serious offences. However, a Black or minority youth can spend several months waiting to be bailed out of detention because a parent who works minimum wage is unable to pay the cost of bail, or the youth was living with a guardian hired by CAS who refuses to offer bail.
6. Community youth engagement groups occur in most major cities across the country. These groups encourage youths to become more involved in their community and reduce their feelings of disconnection.
7. Education sessions are held for the justice sector, including police officers, judges, prosecutors, and program service providers, who will make a difference in building a collaborative community.
8. Yet there continues to be an overrepresentation of Black and minority youths who are incarcerated. Still, there is hope for the future, where closings are planned for some large youth custody facilities.
9. There are courts where only youths are tried, and youth court judges recognize the negative impact of racism and trauma as causes of delinquent behaviours.
10. Due to the closure of some of the private youth custody facilities, some youths are moved very far from their communities. This makes it difficult for families and friends to visit.

The Challenging Adolescent Years of Black and Minority Males

Take a few minutes to reflect.

Do you remember when you were an adolescent (teenager), how you tested the limits, pushed the boundaries, challenged authority, talked back to adults, even your parents, and you thought you knew everything? You were impulsive, reactive, and experimented with sex, drugs, and alcohol? Ultimately, you were creative, had boundless energy, and demonstrated resilience; these are all part of normal adolescent behaviour. Did you take risks, such as not respecting your curfew, not listening, especially to those in authority, and walking and dressing in ways that identified your cultural background?

The teenage years are among the most challenging periods of adjustment in a young person's life. Hormonal changes, combined with increasing expectations, responsibilities, and decisions, often lead to confusion and emotional behaviour. This adjustment period can challenge the entire family dynamic, and parents may often feel that their disciplinary methods are no longer producing the desired results.

It is a period of rapid change, often occurring in rapid succession or simultaneously. Beginning with puberty, a youth undergoes significant physical changes simultaneously. Their capacities for thinking and reasoning begin to mature; their emotional responses become more intense, and their social world expands as peer groups become more important and romantic relationships often begin. While negotiating these changes, young people often grapple with their emerging identities, make important decisions about the future, and face several transitions. Their brain function becomes increasingly efficient and specialized. Yet they often do not consider the consequences of their negative behaviours. They are caught up in the me-versus-me stage of life.

The prefrontal cortex (located directly behind the eyes and forehead) is the area of the brain that undergoes the greatest change during puberty. More than any other part of the brain, this area dictates our personality, goals, and values. The maturation of the frontal cortex is a slow process that takes place throughout adolescence and early adulthood. The prefrontal cortex is referred to as the executive area because it helps to monitor, organize, plan, make decisions, anticipate consequences, control impulses, and delay gratification.

Supporting young people's successful transition to adulthood requires a clear understanding of the predictable stages of their development. While every young person has a unique background, abilities, personal characteristics, life events, and context, major developmental events are common across young people and are likely to occur in the transition from childhood to adulthood.

During this developmental stage, parent-adolescent relationships may suffer. As youths devote their time to peers and perhaps romantic relationships, their connection with their parents can suffer, leading to heightened conflict. Conflicts with parents are most frequent in early to mid-adolescence and generally decline afterwards.

This is often when parents seek professional advice on managing their teens' behaviour. The youths may even report to the school that they do not get along with their parents and no longer want to live at home because of the conflict. This reporting is neither neglect nor abuse. The Children's Aid Society is called, and after investigation and with very little knowledge of the culture, the teen is removed from their home and placed in foster care, where their life becomes a living hell. They find that it is no better than being at home, and that the help required is professional support for the family through conflict-resolution approaches to allow this young person to live with their family.

The privilege of childhood has never been afforded to all children. Society criminalizes normal adolescent behaviours among Black and minority youths more than their White counterparts. The anger develops when children, especially when they are excluded from Western notions of childhood innocence. It has been said that the kids who need love will ask for it in the most unloving ways. The behaviours they demonstrate are an indicator of the help they need.

Black adolescents are discriminated against by teachers and discouraged from taking challenging courses, even when they have stated they would like to try. They are often viewed with suspicion, monitored more heavily, and punished more severely than other students. Black teens who feel overly monitored by their superiors develop tougher demeanours, which leads them into more conflict later in life. They may wear hoodies and, therefore, be criminalized. Wearing their pants below the waist is looked at so negatively that it is said that *they are either coming out of jail, involved in gangs, or just waiting to be arrested.*

One must only visit the youth shelters to find Black youths who have run away from family homes, residential placements, group homes, and foster care because their physical, emotional, and mental health needs are not met in these places. Community resources are required to diagnose and treat mental illness, provide supportive housing, and educate society, especially those who work in the institutions, about racism, racial disparities, and the pervasive stereotypes that are used for differential treatments of Black youth.

Please remember that the adolescent years represent a significant period of experience and opportunity during which all youths explore their world, develop a sense of being, and define their identity. Experiences with racism within the different spaces that Black and minority youths occupy create negative encounters for them.

A Black male adolescent strives to live through these years as best as possible.

A Short Q&A for Parents and Teens

Discuss the responses you know, then research to find the other responses. The answers can also be found in the back pages of this book.

1. Your 13-year-old son told you that he is being bullied at school; what is the first thing you will do?
2. A White teenager hit your son in the face while walking in the park. You saw this interaction; what will you do?
3. Your daughter had many friends in middle school, but when she moved to high school with them, by mid-semester, she had only one friend remaining. How do you address this issue?
4. Your daughter excelled in music during middle school and wants to attend a school of the arts for music education, but the teacher tells you she won't succeed. What will you do?
5. Your daughter excels in math, but she's noticed that when she raises her hand to answer a question in class, the math teacher often ignores her. Is there anything that you can do as a parent?
6. A very good friend of the family tells you that his teenage son was arrested by the police last evening and is going to court later today. How can you help?
7. In a discussion with your two teenage children, they tell you that racism is rampant at their school. What are four things you want to know to provide support for them?

8. A new Black immigrant teen seems very sad in your class. What can you, as a classmate, do to help him?
9. As a teen, a police officer stops you on your way from the grocery store. He tells you that someone looking like you recently robbed the store. What is the first thing you will do?
10. How can parents collaborate with their teens to educate them about prevention?

CHAPTER 3

When Assumptions Become Sentences

Assumptions about Incarcerated Black and Minority Youths

The negative assumptions start long before the youths become involved with the criminal justice system, and thereby, it is the stigmatization and racist acts that cause them to become involved. You have read, heard, or seen a teenager walk into a supermarket to purchase a food item during their lunch break. The security guard at the entrance observed the teen entering the store and then followed him as he made stops throughout the store. Sometimes, it's done blatantly, by walking behind him or observing from a distance. Due to his stereotypical thinking, he assumed that, being a Black male, he was not there to make a purchase but was instead looking to steal an item.

> *Rather than assuming things, make sure you learn the facts.*
> *Before you judge others, try to understand them.*
> *Before you hurt someone, consider how you would feel.*
> *Before you speak out, think about the impact of your words.*
>
> – ***Wisdomtoinspirethesoul.com***

Racist assumptions cause people to look at innocent Black youths as they enter different spaces to see them as criminals. It is also assumed that they are lazy, dishonest, and older than their age, leading to disproportionately negative treatment compared to White youths. Many become angry, especially when they have not learned how to manage these negative encounters. They are fighting for their lives and being smothered with negativity.

It is not anecdotes that inform us about this negative phenomenon; this information is found in our Canadian and American statistics in the twenty-first century. Black youths in Canada are overrepresented in the criminal justice system and experience discrimination and anti-Black racism at every stage.

It is assumed that these young people are criminals because of their Black skin, the way they dress, talk, and interact with others. They are often seen as antisocial and violent. In 2022, a White professor in one of Canada's universities said that she was afraid to teach in her classroom because a Black student who seemed to be over six feet in height appeared as a threat in the classroom.

Canadian Statistics from Three Provinces:

- **Admissions to Correctional Services:** In 2020/21, Black youths made up 10% of youth admissions to correctional services in Nova Scotia, Alberta, and British Columbia, despite representing only 4% of the youth population in those provinces. In Ontario's largest youth secure custody facility on any given day, 90% of the incarcerated youths are Black and other minorities.
- **Admissions to Pre-Trial Detention:** In 2016, Black youths made up 20.6% of admissions to secure pre-trial

detention and 15.3% of admissions to pre-trial detention overall.

- **Sentencing:** Black youths often receive longer sentences than White youths.
- **Bail:** Black youths are more likely to be denied bail than White youths.
- **Mental Health and Social Services:** Black youths are less likely to be referred to mental health programs and other social services than White youths.
- **Jury Selection:** White people are more likely to sit on juries than Black people, which can diminish the consideration of Black youth's histories in decision-making.
- **Experiences in the Correctional System:** Black youths often describe their experiences in the correctional system as dehumanizing, violent, and neglectful.

A Sampling of the Statistics in the United States

For a decade, incarceration disparities between Black and White youth have remained stubbornly high. As of 2021, Black youths were 4.7 times as likely to be placed (i.e., detained or committed) in juvenile facilities as their White peers, according to nationwide data collected in October 2021 and recently released. This disparity has *remained largely unchanged over the past decade.*

Juvenile facilities, including 1,323 detention centers, residential treatment centers, group homes, and youth prisons, held 24,894 youths as of October 2021. (These data do not include the 291 people under 18 in adult prisons at year-end 2021 or the estimated 2,000 people under 18 in adult jails at midyear 2021.)

In 2021, the national youth placement rate was 74 per 100,000. The Black youth placement rate was 228 per 100,000, compared to the White youth placement rate of 49 per 100,000.

Forty-two percent of youths in placement are Black, even though Black Americans comprise only 15% of all youths across the United States. Among all states with a population of at least 8,000 Black youths (between 10 and 17), a cutoff that allows for meaningful comparisons, Black youths are more likely to be in custody than White youths. Black and White youths have similar juvenile placement rates in the District of Columbia.

Many healthcare colleagues said, "Norma, I have no idea how you worked in jail for over five years and continue functioning normally."

I replied, "Help me to understand what that means."

The response is that there are so many negative assumptions, degradation, and dehumanization of incarcerated Black youths that it would be too traumatic to watch the terrible ways in which they are treated.

Does assumption significantly impact the lives of Black youths in negative ways? Research demonstrates that this is one of the main reasons why many of them become involved in the youth criminal justice system. These racialized youths who are experiencing some of the most challenging periods in their lives due to a host of different pressures can lead to poor decision-making, which could solidify the assumptions.

Even when they are incarcerated, they experience a legacy of maltreatment and exposure to dehumanizing situations.

A Lived Experience

Food Dirtied as Retribution

If you were offered a ham and cheese sandwich but observed that the contents had been removed, thrown into the garbage by youth service officers, and replaced with sputum, would you eat it?

While in custody, Michael had been involved in many fights with other youth, especially when they were participating in sports or when dining together in the dining hall. He had been escorted back to his cell quite often and taken to the secure isolation cell as a last resort when youth service officers were unable to subdue him with coaching. He was an irate young Black male who would demonstrate challenging behaviours such as punching, kicking others, swearing, and throwing items. He often spends many days and nights in the locked, secure isolation cell.

Michael was born in a war-torn country. His dad taught him how to use a gun to kill enemies. He lived with his parents and a younger sister in a part of his country where the war was ongoing. His dad took him to the battlefield when he was only eight. During the raging war, he accidentally shot and killed his dad. No words can adequately describe the impact of this agonizing situation on Michael's world. His mother does not recall any specific support for her family in a refugee camp, especially around mental health and negative behaviours.

When he was twelve years old, he, his mother, and his sister arrived directly from a refugee camp in Canada. His mother shared their story with the psychologist who was assigned to his healthcare, stating that his behaviour was difficult to manage, but she did not know where to find resources to help him. She was also grieving the loss of her husband and all her belongings, coming to a new, unfamiliar country where she required ongoing support for herself and her daughter. It was emotionally, physically, and psychologically challenging to adjust to a new country and a different culture, so Michael was given insufficient time. He did not attend school; he roamed the streets while they lived in a shelter in the big metropolitan city.

By the time Michael was thirteen years old, he was picked up by the police for stealing and fighting in public places. They took him back to the shelter many times and informed his mother how to manage his behaviour. He would do so briefly and then return to the street. In one of these fights, he pushed an elderly man off the sidewalk onto the street, where he bumped his head and became unconscious. A passerby called 911, and the elderly man was assessed by paramedics and taken to the hospital. Michael was arrested by the police and taken into secure custody, where he awaited a trial in youth court.

His behaviour heightened when he was moved from a cell to the isolation room. There, for the fourth or fifth time in a month, he had nothing to do but stare at the wall, and at times, he would lie on the concrete floor and look out the window built into the lower half of the door. The youth services officers slid his meal trays through this area of the door, as with all youths placed in secure isolation. Because of his age, stage of development, and past traumatic life experiences, he had limited skills to help him deal with living with others in an institutional structure. He was always hypervigilant and did not trust anyone to be kind to him.

The morning routine at this facility involves the senior management team visiting the youths in secure isolation, then moving around the property to see the others outside that area who reside in the "pods."

One morning, when the door to his secure isolation cell was opened, one of the senior members of the management team said, "We are so tired of you being in this damn cell;" no good morning, nor how are you.

Michael has acted impulsively before, so when he heard that morning's greeting, he reached out and slapped the senior staff across his face. The door was slammed shut immediately, and the senior staff was furious, saying, "Keep him here longer; perhaps he will learn his lesson."

Here are senior personnel who do not realize the harmful, inhuman, cruel, and degrading treatment of a youth being punished in that manner. The negative consequences of using secure isolation to manage the behaviour of youths are not well understood, and given that it is a period of critical brain development in the youth, the use of this kind of punishment with adolescents presents considerable risk. It affects how they see themselves and alters their psychological state. They feel they have lost control.

In Ontario, when a young person is placed in secure isolation, facilities must follow the procedures and complete the forms prescribed in the Youth Justice Services Manual. Statistics shared in a "Systemic Review of Secure Isolation" indicated that in 2013, Ontario's largest secure youth custody facility had an average of 78 youths and recorded 420 placements in secure isolation. (A placement varies from 1 to 72 hours.) Many youths had multiple stays in isolation, not tracked by name. A youth can leave the isolation cell and attend court, and when they return and are placed back in isolation, this is documented as a new admission.

Michael sat on the concrete floor all morning, occasionally looking out to the hallway through the door's small opening, built into the lower part. When the lunch trays arrived, he observed that the trays were given to other youths by sliding them under the doors. He also observed that his tray was on the desk counter. Before the officer slid the tray to him through the slot, he removed the ham and cheese from his sandwich and threw them in the garbage. The two youth services officers on duty each took turns coughing up sputum in the sandwich, closed it, placed it on his tray, and slid it under the door. He picked up the tray and put it on the cot he slept on. He recalled being allowed to speak with a social worker the previous day, and she informed him that wherever he was in the facility, he could ask someone to have her visit him.

Michael waited for a while, then asked the officer to call the social worker to come see him. The social worker came, and she was allowed into his secure cell. He handed her his lunch tray. He asked her to wait until she entered the healthcare department to open it and see the nurse. He began to trust the nurses because they were allowed to administer his required medication, and he developed a trusting relationship with them. Anne, the social worker, opened the door to the healthcare department and walked into my office. Closing the door, she said, "I don't know what to expect, but I think it would be safer if both of us see what is on this tray." We opened what seemed to be a sandwich and found it filled with sputum.

As a part of my lived experience in this institution, when I recall this horrific dehumanization of youth, my head aches, my gut rumbles, and tears are running down my face for this young human being. Though I am no longer in the situation and am only recalling what happened, I can still feel the emotions. He is Black, and I am Black, and there was no process for me to have assisted him out of that inhumane situation. Even as I recall what happened that day, I am so angry that a young person could be treated in this manner. What he did was wrong. There are many other ways to bring to one's attention the wrong that was done and how this could have been remedied without inflicting such harm and trauma.

In my office, the social worker cried silently; we hugged each other. We know that when a youth is held in secure isolation, they are treated very inhumanely. Still, even after reading the literature on youth incarceration, we have not come across this form of cruel treatment. Can you believe that most of our society says to lock them up when they commit crimes so that they will learn their lessons? Of course, they are all Black and minority youth, and an overwhelming number are incarcerated and will not return to their community as a whole person. They will be overly traumatized and left to get revenge on someone else.

I called the senior administrator's office because my direct supervisor was out of the office that day. I requested a short meeting to discuss an incident in the secure isolation area. The social worker and I took the tray to his office and informed him of what had happened. He did not look at the sandwich; he responded, "Take the damn tray out of my office, throw it into the garbage, and have the kitchen make the boy another sandwich." We had no choice; we threw away the tray in the garbage and left.

On our return to my office, we both held hands and prayed for this young man, his family, and the staff who were responsible for his safety in the secure isolation cell. The social worker then called her manager to my office, informed her about the event, and said this would be her last day working there. Anne gave a verbal notice of her resignation. She planned to pack her belongings from a shared office and send her written resignation the following day. We both offered her time off work to seek psychological help, but she refused. She said, "I need to be away from here to feel human again."

She packed her belongings; I walked her to her car, ensuring she could drive the short distance to her home. She drove away from the facilities in her car. I understood from her manager that she did accept psychological support to overcome the traumatic experience and became healthy before being gainfully employed elsewhere.

A Question

Why was this teen detained so long, moving in and out of an isolation cell while he waited to go to court? Could he have asked for financial help to pay for this bail? His life story shows that his mother lived in a shelter, would not have had those funds, and did not know about legal aid. No one in the justice system gave her instructions on how to ask for help to decrease the time her son spent in detention. She had no legal life skills.

Policies in all youth custody facilities are developed in accordance with the YCJA, which directs staff that youths under 16 years must not be kept in solitary isolation for more than 8 hours on any given day or 24 hours a week. A Provincial Director, after reviewing the situation, must approve any youth held for more than 72 hours per week. [*Section 25(1) of the YCJA*]

He was moved back and forth within the policy timeframe. There was no discussion among the managers and the administrators that when a youth spends so much time being confined, it is a serious human rights violation and can constitute a form of cruel punishment.

Did the Administrator know about the alternatives in the Youth Criminal Justice Act, which directs that alternatives be used instead of jail, and why did no other person intervene on his behalf? His mother, a refugee in our country, is already so traumatized by having to live in a shelter in a new country that she would not have known about the alternatives.

This is a Black adolescent who had undergone much trauma; nowhere in his documentation was this considered when he was arrested, locked up, and removed from a single cell to isolation many times. We have heard stories about the deep emotional wound caused by trauma. There is research that shows that toxic stress, which naturally results as a response to frightening or threatening trauma, can derail changes in behaviour, emotional health, and cognitive capacity. This young person's health is compounded by the additional trauma he experienced.

Psychologists work daily in the custody facility and evaluate the health of youth, but only when referrals are made. The psychologist received a referral to see him only when his behaviour worsened. Very few White teenagers are incarcerated for a long time while waiting to go to court. They may experience some trauma, but not over a long time and not in the same way as Black youths do. Their parents become involved and plan ways to get them home until their court date is known. Many times, the parents of these Caucasian youth, through their lawyers, can agree on an alternative to house arrest.

Sadly, instead of providing trauma support for this Black teen, he was viewed as a troublemaker. These harmful assumptions and stereotypes of Black youths manifest anti-Black racism in numerous ways. It usually compromises their mental health, well-being, sense of identity, and potential adverse outcomes for release back into the community.

Eventually, the administrator and his senior team arranged for the youth's transfer out of the facility.

If I were a fly on the wall in the Administrator's office, I would see him pick up the phone, speak to his director at the Ministry, and say, "We are moving this boy, Michael. He needs to be transferred out to a smaller facility where they can teach him lessons of obedience."

The next day, the youth was not seen at the facility. He was transferred out overnight to a smaller secure custody facility many miles away from his family. This is another form of retribution and punishment over which the youth and his family have no control. His mother can no longer visit or call him because of the distance. The folks who make assumptions about Black male youth do not reflect on how they are setting them up to fail. They would rather see them being incarcerated than living in the community, where there could be opportunities to access mental healthcare for their well-being and success.

Teaching Michael "a lesson" in a smaller institution could worsen his life. There is no daily access to healthcare and programs for healing from trauma. He could spend a longer time in isolation because the small custody facility does not have an adequate number of staff to assist him in understanding or managing his disruptive behaviour.

Assumptions are made, even at this stage, that a smaller facility would be a better placement where he would receive more punishment than rehabilitation. All forms of inequality and injustice are most shocking and inhumane.

Research has shown that there is ongoing unfair treatment of Black and minority youths as they try to navigate the youth criminal justice system. Assumptions override how they are seen. They are criminals, and removing them from society demands that they experience punishment while they are incarcerated for their criminal activities.

CHAPTER 4

Systems, Stigma, & Their Cost

The Systems of Oppression and Marginalization

Despite the national pride that Canada holds as a multicultural country, open to all cultures, races, and ethnicities, there remain undercurrents of anti-Black racism that persist throughout this country. They are due to systemic and institutional policies that have led to unfounded beliefs resulting in race-based trauma and psychological wounds, which negatively impact Black families.

Black and minority communities continue to live with the effects of prejudice, discrimination, repeated trauma, and hatred. Most Black families have said that they have experienced racial discrimination (75%), either regularly (13%) or from time to time (62%). They report that these experiences make them feel like the system is set up to fail them. They also feel that they must work harder than everyone else to achieve success. Black families include youths who reported that these systems of oppression shape how they see themselves and were designed to keep them down.

Why do we see so many Black and Minority male youths being over-incarcerated? The way they are viewed in the following five central systems of oppression and marginalization has a profoundly negative impact on their lives.

Societal Oppression and Marginalization

Society's harmful oppression and marginalization of racialized youths are routinely stereotyped as foreigners or immigrants, even when they and their parents are born in North America. It is often said that they do not belong to American or Canadian culture, regardless of their citizenship or immigration status. This is one of the baselines that informs the assumptions of White educators that poor educational outcomes and disciplinary problems are a result of their foreign cultures and their presumed inability or unwillingness to assimilate.

When society fails to help our children reach their potential, it wants the problems solved by locking them up in jail.

The mainstream understanding of the criminal justice system is that it picks up the most dangerous individuals in society. It targets the attention of the criminals and protects the victims. Aspects of our culture see the justice system as finding those who have committed crimes and incarcerating them to facilitate their removal from society. I have heard this said by hundreds of individuals, who added that society would be safer and that young people could learn valuable lessons when punished and taught to behave normally while in jail. The idea is that a young Black person, no matter their culture, cannot master their fate to achieve more in society.

Living within a society that is organized based on a skin colour hierarchy creates a complex set of challenges for adolescents of colour. Many teens have some insecurities about not fitting in; these feelings are often intensified for teens of colour, who very frequently receive powerful, rejecting messages based on their race and the colour of their skin.

One of the implications of racialization is that it blames victims for their circumstances. It takes away from examining the various systemic, structural, and institutional forms of oppression that function to ensure that racialized and minoritized bodies remain in inferior positions for the benefit of colonization.

These discussions also fail to take into consideration the systemic forces of racism, prejudice, discrimination, addiction, mental illness, and the operation of White privilege. Blacks and minorities who suffer in poverty, unemployment, and precarious immigration status, and who live in low-income housing, are seen as suffering from deficiencies in their lifestyles or possessing personal inadequacies. It is increasingly clear, then, that the reason for the plight of these young persons of colour is due to the systemic forces they encounter. If the community is viewed in this way, so are the young people from those communities.

I carried out two small random samplings where I asked each person from a variety of nationalities, whom I encountered at a craft market and a church, "What should be done with young Black and minority youths who commit crimes? How should society respond to these young people when they become involved with the youth justice criminal system?"

One sample comprised 20 individuals of mixed race, and the other comprised 10, mostly Whites. Of the 30 individuals, 29 said to lock them up until they learn their lessons, and one person said they are kids; look at where they come from and help them change their lives. This is precisely what is happening in our society, where the colour of one's skin defines and explains behaviours and approaches used for correction. Responses from 99% of individuals in this random sample, which contained many ethnic persons, including Black adults, said it is best to incarcerate young people when they demonstrate delinquent behaviours in any setting.

Not many realize that social conditions in some neighbourhoods, including a lack of space for residents to meet and socialize, can lead to disorganization and a retreat from public spaces, thereby making those neighbourhoods unsafe. The Province of Ontario, built low-income housing where many folks live in poverty, are unemployed, and lack many life skills.

There are few open spaces for youths living in Ontario housing to actively socialize in, and even the small outdoor spaces are often monitored by security or police officers. They gather in the stairways and the lanes between apartment buildings and are then seen as collaborating on criminal activities. Seen in these places by the public, they are brought to the attention of the justice system.

Decades of evidence have left no doubt that locking up youths harms their future and does little to protect public safety. There must be better ways to protect young people from becoming involved in the justice system.

It will take extensive education and advocacy to assist individuals in understanding the impact of racism and how Black youths are impacted. All youth, regardless of their background, have a presence in society; they belong here. Society has failed them by not taking responsibility to make a difference. Not only do parents love their children, but some Black families strive to go beyond society's expectations to love all children, so they feel valued and equipped to reach their potential.

Some think that Black and minority youths commit more crimes than White youths when they live in low-income settings. What they fail to realize is that structural racism plays a significant role in who is charged with crimes, who is convicted, and who serves a sentence.

A Different Approach to White vs. Black Youth on the Street

Society supports and says that Black and marginalized youths should not be on the street at night. They are planning to steal, murder, or break into residences or businesses. They are often not seen as doing as well as White youth.

Two youths were standing at the bus stop late at night, on their return from extracurricular activities in the community; one was Black and the other White. A police officer stops his patrol car and asks, "Where are you going?" Both say, heading home. However, the Black youth resembled someone who had participated in a robbery earlier, so he was detained by the officer, who posed several questions. Right or wrong, this youth gets defensive and speaks up about his rights. The officer sees this as disrespectful and charges him with assault, and he is escorted to jail. The White youth boarded the bus and went home unscathed.

Our police services are an intricate part of our society, and some do a great job in the prevention and management of Black and minority youths to prevent them from being incarcerated. Others view them as criminals even when they do not harm. They are seen as inherently more criminal due to a combination of racial profiling, implicit bias, and historical stereotypes that associate Blackness with criminality.

Though this was a policing issue, the media reported that a Black youth assaulted an officer when asked why he was out late at night.

Media's Oppression and Marginalization

The media plays a role in racism by influencing public attitudes and shaping their opinions. Some news stories about crimes committed by Black and minority youths are sensationalized as violent acts and express "sadness" that the public cannot be informed about the name and age of the youth, along with more details of what led to the crime.

They fail to take the time to understand the YCJA because the news is so sensationalized, and the public must know who these young criminals are.

It is often the day's headline news. Some entertainment frequently features negative images and stereotypes of Black and minority youth. It usually leads to the broader role of in-depth racism in our society when these snap judgements are made.

These dominant narratives of the media covering youth violence often omit to discuss systemic inequities and practices that perpetuate the social circumstances in high-priority neighbourhoods, such as a lack of timely access to mental healthcare, resources to purchase healthy food, and low-paying jobs. Instead, the media blames social problems on the people who live in those communities. Often, when racialized youths commit crimes, the narrative emerges that these are bad kids who continue to make poor choices.

Some media sources want to see a tough-on-crime approach for racialized youths, where the courts should be considering adult sentences for youths convicted of serious crimes, restricting probation, community diversion programs, and allowing the publication of the names and ages of these youths.

A tough-on-crime approach does not reduce crime. Society should instead support measures to prevent youth violence by using the legislation in the Youth Justice Criminal Act and investing in social programs and community initiatives. Join forces to look at the root causes of crimes committed by racialized youths and focus on primary prevention rather than intervention after a crime has been committed.

According to Statistics Canada, almost 63,000 people in Ontario identify as Black or African Canadian. Black refers to a diverse group of people from various ethnicities, backgrounds, and identities. Despite this diversity, Black Ontarians share a common African heritage, a common history of colonialism and slavery, and, consequently, the typical day experience of anti-Black racism, resulting in socioeconomic, health, educational, and social disparities.

Anti-Black racism is a term that describes the beliefs, attitudes, prejudices, damaging stereotypes, and discrimination of people of African descent. These beliefs and attitudes are held by individuals and are also embedded in the policies and practices of many.

Anti-black racism negatively impacts how African Canadians are treated when accessing many services. The web of anti-Black racism hinders equitable access to services and contributes to poor outcomes for Black children, youth, and families. (*Review of Promising Practices: Supports for Black Parents, 2020*)

Abundant research shows that most people's thinking is swayed by subconscious attitudes that lead them to view and respond to people of colour differently from Whites. The impact of this form of racism is powerful in perpetuating disparities in the juvenile justice system. Overt racism is the easiest to see, unlike the less obvious or more hidden forms of racism known as covert racism. Overt racism is the intentional and/or obvious harmful attitudes or behaviours toward another minority individual or group because of their skin colour.

The Healthcare System's Oppression and Marginalization

In the community, many cultures face challenges in accessing timely healthcare, particularly those residing in rural areas and low-income settings. One can only imagine how much harder it is for Black adolescents to access healthcare promptly. These challenges are due to the impact of racism and discrimination within the healthcare system. It takes a physical and emotional toll on Black people and minorities.

Racism is a socially transmitted illness that should be a significant public health concern, but it is often not seen as such. Racism is incredibly prevalent, and some medical personnel may not support the youth and family who report that it is racism that caused a decline in the youth's mental well-being. To complicate the problem further, Black and minority people are less likely to have adequate access to medical care or are poorly treated when they do seek help. They have difficulty locating healthcare professionals who are culturally sensitive to the issues they are struggling with. Young people often avoid healthcare due to concerns about confidentiality and stigma, and are less likely to discuss sensitive information.

There is also a lack of representation in the healthcare field. Black youths would like to share how they are feeling with someone who looks like them and is likely to understand the challenge from a cultural viewpoint. There is such stigma about mental illness that an adolescent often has to be convinced by a parent or trusted guardian that he is unwell emotionally and psychologically before he would tell his story to a specialist. If the professional is White, this can cause hesitation due to cultural aspects and a fear that the information may not remain confidential.

There are also financial issues. In Ontario, a youth has a mental assessment on entering youth custody and has a psychiatric follow-up within 72 hours. Having a mental illness is not a crime, yet our institutions are locking up young persons with mental illness, rather than providing adequate healthcare resources in the community. A first referral in the community will result in an assessment, but follow-up visits require payment. If you have no money, you remain unwell with heightened mental health needs until your behaviour cannot be managed in the community. You are then sent to a hospital where you are provided with an assessment, given medications, and perhaps discharged to the community to begin the cycle again.

Pain Management: I worked as a healthcare leader in the youth criminal justice sector. Even when the youths are secluded in a custody environment, their access to healthcare is often delayed. I had to fight "like hell" to ensure appropriate healthcare was delivered to Black and minority youths when the requests were filtered through youth service officers. So many racist attitudes boggle the mind. They do not feel pain as Whites do; their skin is black and thicker, and they always seek drugs because they are all druggies and report fake pain. Why would anyone with horrific pain, such as wounds inflicted by gunshots, or large open wounds that occur while climbing over a barbed wire fence to escape being arrested, or the sickling of one's red blood cells, be considered feigning pain?

I felt nauseated as I watched Black youths wreathed in pain, along with being humiliated due to the colour of their skin. Their voices are nullified, and they become angry because they are seen as unworthy of receiving timely healthcare. Because of such systemic barriers in accessing healthcare, they are predisposed to worse health outcomes compared to White adolescents. When access to physical healthcare is such a challenge, it is more difficult to access mental healthcare. According to a report by the Mental Health Commission of Canada (MHCC, 2021) titled "Shining a light on Mental Health in the Black communities in Canada," between 2001 and 2014, 38.3% of Black Canadian residents with poor or fair self-reported mental health used mental health services, compared with 50.8% of White Canadian residents with similar concerns.

Quick Facts about Mental Illness in Adolescents

Research has identified that a significant proportion of youths within the justice system possess some form of mental health disorder, and that the presence of an emotional disorder provides an explanatory value regarding the cause of crime. The percentage may be as high as one-fifth or 20% of those who have a diagnosis of a mental health disorder. (*Longwoods.com, Quarterly 2011*)

The mental illnesses that most commonly affect adolescents can be as follows, and are a mere sample of many more:

- Anxiety disorder, which manifests through fears, phobias, worry, and nervous conditions

- Depressive disorders – characterized by states of hopelessness or helplessness
- Bipolar disorder
- Conduct disorder
- Several eating disorders
- Childhood schizophrenia

Brief Points on Mental Health in Black Adolescents:

1. Black youths are more likely to access mental healthcare for the first time through the Justice System or emergency department, and they wait longer for mental healthcare than any other population in Canada. (*Government of Canada, Mental Health Report, 2021*)
2. 38.3% of Black Canadian residents with poor or self-reported mental illness used mental health services compared with 50.8% of White Canadian residents. (*Between 2001 and 2004; Mental Health Commission, 2021*)
3. A 2020 report showed that among Black Caribbean populations, wait times for mental healthcare averaged 16 months, whereas wait times for White populations averaged seven months. (*Mental Health Commission, 2021*)
4. Despite the higher prevalence of mental illness found in low-income areas (where Black populations disproportionately reside), these communities often have fewer mental health programs and services. (*Mental Health Commission, 2021*)

Many Black and minority youths have suffered complex trauma repeated in various forms of victimization, racism in the schools, life-threatening accidents, and interpersonal loss at an early age. Were you aware that a Black or minority young person who was left at an early age in their country of birth and lived with a grandparent for several years experienced intense trauma when the opportunity arose for that youth to immigrate to Canada?

On arrival in Canada, parents have very high expectations for their future and neglect to address the issues of moving to a new country where they do not know all the norms, miss family and friends, and are expected to adhere to new rules in the new home. Some have difficulty coping with high levels of stress, inability to focus on learning new skills, feelings of being lost, show impulsiveness, and maladaptive ways of surviving.

As any parent, youth worker, or young adult can verify, mental illness in adolescence may be characterized by a roller coaster of emotional and psychological highs and lows. Intense feelings are a normal and healthy part of the psychological landscape of youth. It is also true that many mental health disorders of adulthood begin in childhood or adolescence. A mental health disorder can disrupt daily functioning in the home, school, or community. Many parents do not recognize the early onset of a mental illness in their children, and without early intervention, it takes much longer to restore health.

The stigma of having a mental illness prevents most families from seeking healthcare for themselves or their children. Under-representation of Black service providers, such as physicians, psychologists, and psychiatrists, to whom Black persons can relate and share their health challenges. Studies have shown that ethnic matching of service providers and patients generally increases utilization and reduces dropout rates.

There are times when Black parents assume that their teenagers are lazy when they do not want to go to school, drop out of school, or are not eager to participate in social activities. The impact of anti-racism does show up in this manner and could have been the environmental cause for the onset of the mental illness. Not all physicians, clinics, and hospitals can meet the needs of culturally diverse groups. Young Black people often say, “I am misunderstood; they do not understand my culture, where you are told to ‘man it up’ and work through your illness.”

By the time some of our Black and minority youths are diagnosed, they are suffering through trauma and have become severely ill. They act out in many negative ways, such as becoming involved with drug dealings to calm their minds and to earn money to purchase additional amounts of drugs. These activities lead them to engage in criminal activities, such as stealing.

Have you ever heard a Black parent say, “We don’t have time to feel anxious or get depressed? We have too much work to do and too many situations to manage at our children’s school, in the workplace, and even in family dramas.” It takes everything in a Black person to keep life going, and they may miss some of the signs of mental illness in themselves and their children. The over-representation of Black and minority youths in the justice system who present with undiagnosed mental illness clearly shows various reasons why this occurs.

Many are lacking timely access to informed, sensitive, and culturally competent healthcare. Some will not discuss their mental status because of the stigma that they may encounter. As a nurse, I know physicians who say to young people, “What do you mean by feeling depressed? Just get to bed on time, get up, go to school, and learn for your future. You have nothing to worry about; you have a home, loving parents, and three meals a day. It’s up to you to get going!” Most of these healthcare professionals do not carry out mental health assessments in their offices, nor do they know some of the signs and symptoms of mental illness in young Black persons.

CHAPTER 5

Lessons That Cost Lives

Oppression and Marginalization in the School System

It produces a pipeline to incarceration for Black and Minority youth.

Public Education is the most critical investment that countries make for their future. It should be a tangible expression for society. Schools profoundly influence how students understand themselves and the roles and responsibilities they are expected to fulfill. What if you are Black and marginalized, and you do not always feel that you belong and are allowed to thrive? The best and most authentic version of who we are and how we relate to the world plays a significant role in schools. Children learn to foster their identity and build a sense of belonging, yet some schools do not facilitate these goals. (*We are what we teach, Aspen Institute, 2023*)

The "Ontario Education Act" is provincial legislation that establishes the legal framework for education in the province. The act informs us about the roles of the education minister and school boards, the responsibilities of principals and teachers, the rights and responsibilities of families and their children, and other key aspects of our education system. Any child living in the province of Ontario has the right to attend school from age 6 to 18. They have this right even if their parents are not Canadian citizens or do not have legal status in Canada. A few exceptions exist, such as individuals visiting with their children or homeschooling by parents or students who are identified as international and must pay a fee. If parents fall into the category of parents whose children should be in school but are not, they could be charged with their child's truancy.

Schools are sites of contention for Black youths and their families, where they experience painful everyday racism from educators, administrators, and their peers. Issues of racial inequity within Ontario's education system and, more specifically, the presence of anti-Black racism. These issues have been researched and documented for over forty years.

1. The erasure of Black history and Black excellence in the curriculum. (In some instances, it was never included.)
2. Race-based streaming practices limit the youth from pursuing post-secondary education and meaningful careers. In September 2023, the Ontario Ministry of Education Report eliminated streaming in secondary schools, but it has not provided substantial support for students to pursue other educational endeavours.
3. The under-representation of Black Ontarians among educators and school trustees denies Black youths an essential source of informal guidance and role modelling.
4. A lack of trust between Black students and school staff.
5. High rates of disciplinary actions against Black youth, such as suspensions and expulsions.

6. Low expectations of Black students' academic performance undermine Black youths' notions of what is possible in their education and their careers. (*Source: www.youthrex.com*)

Thanks to a few excellent teachers/educators and other professionals who mentor and support Black and minority children in reaching their full potential despite all these systemic barriers. We need more of you! We must remember that teachers are themselves parents; they find their jobs stressful, and we must help lay the foundations for effective learning. Where I am today, I stand in honour on the shoulders of one of my teachers, Mrs. Livingston, who validated, affirmed, and walked beside me every step to allow me to reach my potential.

Mind you, there are teachers, for whatever reason, even though they are Black, who do not take the time to provide support and positive role modelling for Black children. Next is an example of just that. I spoke at an organization's annual general meeting on the topic of ways society can help our Black children become valued members of our communities. I expressed how children can be disadvantaged when they are living in the custody of the Children's Aid Society, instead of parents being taught and supported to care effectively for their children.

A Black high school principal in the audience came outside the room and said, "I would like to talk with you." I listened, and she informed me that some of these Black children are cared for better within the public system than in their homes. Would you like your child to attend a school where this principal plays such an important role in developing her staff and students? She is unaware of the children who live in foster care, who receive their care in hotel rooms and motels. I was so astonished that a Black principal would verbalize such negative words!

Once I managed to respond, I said, “You have assimilated and, therefore, have become a part of the problem. You also do not seem to understand the systemic barriers that contribute to racial discrimination, often in ways that may not always be immediately visible but have long-term consequences. You need to demonstrate empathy for all children in your school.”

She briskly walked away. I view such an educator as someone who lacks cultural competencies regarding the multifaceted experiences of Black students. I imagine that in her school, Black children are not effectively supported nor enjoy the relationships of teachers, students, and family to achieve learning success. How very sad for the Black students who often search for role models within their cultures. A few Black educators think that they are better off when they realign with White colleagues, measuring their standards against White standards and competing against each other. The oppressed become the oppressor; they need to check themselves.

We must speak up for these children’s rights. Many are lost at school due to racism, expulsion, and suspension, which play a role in banishing them from school. It is imperative that, as a society, we recognize that racism is not solely about the intention but also about the reactions and the consequences it produces for students. Many students are even lost within the classroom setting because they cannot learn, feeling neither validated nor welcomed for who they are. Others are lost because they have precarious immigration status, through no fault of their own, and are not involved in building future careers due to their status.

Over the years, the schools have become an increasingly carceral experience for Black and minority children. Black children from pre-kindergarten through grade 12 are over-represented in every form of discipline, from teacher-issued referrals, suspensions, expulsions, children's aid involvement, and police arrests.

Black students often have their first experiences with the criminal justice system while in school. They feel discriminated against by their teachers and discouraged from taking challenging courses. They are often viewed with suspicion, monitored more heavily, and punished more severely than other students. They demonstrate higher rates of leaving school before graduating, lower post-secondary enrollment rates, and are overrepresented in precarious work when they begin employment. Students who feel overly monitored by their superiors develop tougher demeanours, which leads them into more conflict later in life, strengthening the school-to-prison pipeline. (*Department of Justice, Laidlaw Foundation Report, 2023*)

A Toronto District School Board report stated that during the high school years of Black students, through excessive policing, 42% of these students have been suspended at least once, compared to 18% of non-racialized students. Black students drop out of high school at twice the rate of non-racialized students, 20% versus 11%. Approximately 43% of Black students did not apply to a university. Unsurprisingly, facing excessive policing and racial discrimination throughout their school years can also negatively impact Black students as they enter post-secondary education and the workforce. While they aspire to obtain a university degree, due in part to the lack of support they received in school, they are also less likely than their non-racialized peers to believe they can get one. In a 2016 survey, 94% of Black youths aged 15-25 said they would like to earn a bachelor's degree or higher, but only 60% believed they could. (*Toronto Metropolitan University, 2021*)

The presence of these children remains unwelcome and undesirable in many public schools, and police officers closely monitor their movements. Both the Toronto District School Board and the Peel District School Board discontinued the services of these officers at schools in 2019 after community groups, school board trustees, and students shared their negative experiences. While a few participants had positive things to say about the program, many felt that students of minority backgrounds were under surveillance and intimidation, and felt very uncomfortable with police officers who were roaming their hallways.

Some did not feel safe because they felt that at any minute, if there was disagreement with a fellow student or even with a teacher, instead of being sent to have a follow-up with the principal or the guidance counsellor, the police would become involved, thereby giving them a *police record* which could easily be used against them in the future. One student said, "Having a police record for talking back to a teacher is like living in a police state."

Robyn Maynard noted in her book "Policing Black Lives" that there is a (mis)-education of Black children. Montreal-based Black youths frequently report being treated by teachers as if they are in a gang solely because of their skin colour. School and security staff often dissuade them from gathering in groups to talk, subjecting them to heightened surveillance and frequent identity checks.

In a place where children get socialized and educated, experiencing this typecasting and demonization is deeply harmful to Black youths in their formative years. The feelings of exclusion and pain cause emotional harm and limit their ability to thrive in the school environment. Black youths are exposed to a hostile environment in which they undergo psychological damage, emotional pain, and personal humiliation due to racially discriminatory treatment.

This persistent racial discrimination in schools not only interrupts young Black children's learning ability but also impacts their sense of self, making many of them feel they are not smart enough to belong in formal learning institutions. We know what happens to those who are unable to bear the burden of racism and walk away from school. In the long run, they become despondent, depressed, and involved with the wrong groups, therefore ending up in the youth criminal justice system.

The pipeline from school to jail must be closed and become a pipeline from school to success in the community. We must stop funneling our children from classrooms into the criminal justice system. It should be true that all young Canadians, regardless of race, gender, ethnicity, or socio-economic background, benefit equally from the Canadian education system. Black and other minority youths face systemic and institutional barriers in formal learning that have a long-term impact on their academic, personal, psychological, and social growth.

For decades, Black advocates and families have fought for a more inclusive and equitable education system for Black children. The system of education was founded on colonial principles that did not include Black people but was built to educate Black families toward an understanding of their inferiority. We see where Black children are profiled as troublemakers, and families have much difficulty accessing specialized programs for their children, with low expectations and negative perceptions from teachers, and higher levels of suspension and expulsion than any other group.

Have you heard about the Black children who are suspended while in school? Their education levels are not recognized, and they are not seen as smart, so they are placed in classes with nothing to learn. They sit in class, and if there is no advocate, their next move is to drop out of school. Some teachers have very low expectations of Black students. Their interactions with students create self-doubt, leading students to believe they do not have the academic acumen to attend college or university.

A Canadian study conducted in 2021 found that low-income Black male students experience higher dropout rates compared to their White peers, with many struggling to complete their high school education. Findings show that this was due to the stereotypical understanding of these young men's masculinity, coupled with their race. Those who completed high school have faced many disruptions to their learning due to anti-Black racism and gender biases, and they leave high school with low comprehension levels.

In Ontario, the system that was used to stream mostly Black and minority students has now been stopped by the present government (2022). They were being streamed in Grade 9, away from academically focused classes, because they were not seen as academically inclined. Some are seen as athletes, constructed as misfits, or misbehaving and needing control. Their experiences of being watched and disciplined differ from those of their White counterpart. Black youth, particularly because the identity that is so important to them, are very aware of the way that they are constructed and the way other races are constructed. They feel like outcasts in the school system. They are made to feel they don't belong.

De-streaming is an educational approach that supports achieving equitable outcomes for every learner. Students will not select from the Academic or Applied streams when choosing their courses in Grade 9. Most students entering Grade 9 are to take courses designed for all learners. De-streamed, academic, and open courses will prepare students for university and college – apprenticeship and workplace pathways – providing more post-secondary options. De-streaming is one step toward addressing systemic discrimination and helping break down the barriers for Indigenous, Black, and racialized students, those from low-income housing, those with disabilities, and students with special education needs to maintain equitable opportunities for their future.

Within the education system, according to Robyn Maynard's report in her book *Policing Black Lives*, recent immigrants and refugees are at a higher risk of dropping out, failing, being suspended, expelled, or being streamed into non-academic courses. Black immigrant parents have an essential role in mitigating the effects of anti-Black racism on the development and success of their children. It includes advocating for their children and maintaining good communication with the teachers and school administrators. Parents are encouraged to engage with teachers to ensure their children are progressing well and are supported to succeed.

Black families also struggle to protect their children from the impact of anti-Black racism they experience in the school system. Some parents are unaware of their key rights in the education system, and knowing these rights helps them address issues. Knowing your rights as students and parents is very important. It helps with empowerment, understanding, and the ability to advocate for your children in the face of discrimination. Without this knowledge, taking meaningful actions become difficult. These rights include:

- **The right to appeal** school decisions they believe are unfair, harmful, or discriminatory (as outlined in the Education Act 1990).
- **The right to access information** about their child's education, including academic progress, social development, and their overall well-being at school.

Ontario's public education system is supposed to educate all children equally and prepare them to be confident and competent adults; schools are also the sites in which anti-Black racism is reproduced and perpetuated against Black children. (*Robyn Maynard, Policing Black Lives, 2017*)

Teachers/educators and school staff: please find solutions to engage our Black students. Educators, please uphold principles of fairness and equitable treatment for all students. Please do not exacerbate the difficulties they face by improving the social and educational climate within schools; replace the counterproductive overuse of expulsion and suspension; and provide students with the support they need to maintain good attendance and thrive academically, remaining on track to graduate. Foster success, promote equity, and conform to best practice. Do recognize the realities of adolescent behaviours and brain development, as well as trauma.

Become aware that parenting is quite challenging and that Black folks value the input from the schools. Whether Black parents immigrated to Canada or were born here, they want their children to excel in school. It is an overwhelming burden on parents as they navigate and work their way through the education system in Ontario.

We can no longer band-aid our country's preschool-to-prison pipeline, which pushes children out of the education system and criminalizes them for relatively minor offences.

Do all parents know how to navigate the processes in the school institutions? No! The system is not neutral. Black and minority students are suspended or expelled for things that White students would have done and have the opportunity for warnings. It is caused by racial disparities in disciplining, which lead to substantial disruptions, including the widening of the gap in academic achievement. These disciplinary disparities are better explained by the behaviours of teachers, assistant principals, and principals than by student misconduct or socio-economic status.

Less severe infractions make up most disciplinary referrals to the school office, but teachers refer Black and White students differently for the same misbehaviours. Research has found that White students are referred for objective misdemeanours such as smoking, vandalism, leaving without permission, and obscene language. Black students are referred for subjective misdemeanours such as defiance of authority, disrespect, excessive noise, and loitering. (*Richard O. Welsh, 2021*)

Some intervention strategies involve comprehensive exercises that center on youths and their concerns, interests, and leadership. Reject the notion of disenfranchised youths by defining them as having deficit-based conditions. Best practices are based on a holistic approach to interventions rooted in the communities our youths belong to and on providing wraparound services to meet their multiple cultural needs. Holistic approaches foster collaboration across youth support networks and improve their lives.

Developing effective policies requires articulating a clear vision and commitment to long-term outcomes that are grounded in best practices and measurable. It must also include a concept of well-being, such as physical, emotional, and spiritual health. All these approaches must include families, children, and youths to achieve better outcomes and support their success across all communities.

A recent report, documented in November 2023 by the Laidlaw Foundation, in collaboration with researchers and a youth advisory committee, outlines many measures to achieve effective educational outcomes for Black students and calls on all levels of government to implement them.

1. Provide equitable distribution of education funding and direct additional resources to schools and districts that serve marginalized communities to address disparities and improve educational outcomes.
2. Implement a culturally responsive and inclusive curriculum accurately reflecting Black history, culture, and contributions to Canada.
3. Provide ongoing anti-racist training for educators to address classroom bias and discrimination, and to foster an inclusive and supportive learning environment.
4. Implement strategies to reduce the school-to-prison pipeline by practising restorative justice, positive behaviour interventions, and de-escalation techniques.
5. Increase diversity in the teaching workforce and school leadership to provide positive role models for all students.

6. Address the disproportionate discipline and suspension rates for Black students by implementing alternative disciplinary approaches that prioritize understanding and support over punitive measures.
7. Foster meaningful engagements with families, students, and their communities in educational decision-making processes.

Note: These call-to-action items focused on indigenous students who had experiences similar to those of Black students in the school system.

Children's Aid Society in Ontario

It is titled the Children's Aid Society, but it is the Ontario Child Welfare System for African Canadians.

For many years, the Child Welfare System has been mandated to protect the province's most vulnerable children and youths from abuse and neglect. In keeping with their motto of "working together to keep children safe," there is also a duty to report, which means if anyone has a reason to believe that a child needs protection from abuse or neglect, or a child is at risk of harm, a call must be made to the Children's Aid Society to facilitate a follow-up investigation. However, race matters in the Child Welfare System. The reasons for the disproportionality are multifaceted and complex.

There is a gross over-representation of Black youths and children in the Child Welfare Systems in Ontario. It is reported that 65% of the children and youths in the care of the Children's Aid Society in the greater Toronto area are African Canadian. Yet African Canadians make up only 6.9% of Toronto's population, and just 8% of the city's population is under the age of 18. Contrastingly, 37% of children in care in Toronto are White, while more than 50% of the city's population under 18 is White.

According to research documented by Turner Consulting Group (2019), Black children are often disproportionately represented in the Child Welfare System, not because Black parents are more likely to abuse their children, but because Black families are more likely to be reported to Child Welfare and investigated. Anti-racism affects who is reported, who is investigated, and the outcomes of investigations. Black children are also most likely to be removed from their homes and taken into the care of the Child Welfare System.

This separation from their families causes childhood trauma. It weakens the family bonds and the ongoing support children require as they age. Children who "age" out of the Child Welfare System are more likely to experience low academic achievement, higher unemployment, higher rates of homelessness, housing insecurity, early parenthood, higher criminal justice involvement, and poorer physical and mental health.

In another study conducted by the steering committee of One Vision, One Voice in 2016, the system requires major changes to address this mandate effectively. "No 15-year-old should feel that they have nobody in this world. It was almost the end of me. I thought suicide was better than this life," stated a youth who was taken into CAS without his consent.

Fundamental changes to the Child Welfare System are long overdue because of the negative impact on African Canadian children and their families; systemic racist processes have long buffered this trend, where minority families' cultural practices about their parenting skills are interpreted with bias in a Canadian context. These misinterpretations make families more likely to be scrutinized and subjected to unfounded interventions by Child Welfare. Canada's immigration policies and practices lead to the failed reunification of families and contribute to the large numbers of Black Children "housed" in the Child Welfare System and, in turn, to the over-representation of Black youths in the Youth Justice Criminal System.

In 2011, there were 539,205 African Canadians in Ontario, making up 4% of the provincial population. Statistics Canada projects that the African population could double by 2031. African Canadian children are over-represented in care at five times their representation in the population. There are no significant differences in the overall incidence of child maltreatment between Whites and people of African descent. However, professionals and individuals are more likely to report people of African descent than Whites to Child Welfare. Not only is this heightened observance of African Canadian children, but they are also investigated twice as often as Whites.

There are biases from some teachers who do not understand the cultural practices of African Canadian students, and they may call Child Welfare about a concern with a Black student instead of talking with the parents. Some may fear these parents, and this leads to an over-reporting of these children to the Child Welfare System. Some of these reports are considered "trite" or silly. For example, if a child brings a lunch to school that the teacher is not familiar with (Jamaican patty), if a parent is occasionally late picking up a child, or even if a child uses dramatic language such as "My mom is going to kill me for my low grades," the teacher may call the Child Welfare. Many teachers think that Black parents are too strict with their children or speak too harshly to them. For some, they do not understand why Black parents need to be strict to keep their kids safe in a society that views them as threatening.

A Black teen reported that he was in his high school class and did not want to participate in that day's discussion. His teacher asked him what was wrong, and he responded that he and his family were not getting along and that he was having difficulty learning. The teacher sent him to the principal's office, where a phone call was made to the Child Welfare System. A social worker from the agency arrived quickly to ask the youth questions and took him into the care of the Child Welfare System.

A new immigrant from the Caribbean, he had very strict rules from his parents about attending school, getting home on time, and not wandering in any of the neighbourhoods. When the parents were allowed to share this information with the agency staff, they were told, "This is Canada, and your teen needs some say in his upbringing." It may be true, but is this the best way to share information with a parent and provide support? With help from their community, they could take their son home. Further support was provided by the youth pastor at their church to facilitate conflict resolution approaches within the family structure.

We have lost count of how many times people have asked why the Child Welfare System is broken. The response is that the system was not built to meet the needs of Black and minority families and their children. A system that truly improves the welfare of children would, first and foremost, provide support to the child's family instead of simply reacting to one situation after another with little conceptualization of how their actions have impacted Black and minority families. Communities will always have situations where parents need help raising their children.

Black families have become the focus of the Child Welfare System. Institutionalized legislation requires professionals to report suspected abuse and neglect. Some of the negative consequences are children languishing in foster homes and being moved to several homes over short periods, because we can't manage the misbehaviours. When these behaviours escalate due to multiple reasons such as anger, trauma, hopelessness, and mental illness, the police are called, and they end up in the Youth Justice Criminal System, making it easier to terminate parental rights and lead these youths down the path of no return.

This complex system is to protect children from abuse, but the system comprises children who have not experienced abuse. Rather, they have experienced racism, discrimination, and poverty, and witnessed parental substance use or domestic violence. The system tries to find them a better family that aligns with White middle-class values, norms, and resources. Acting in the child's best interest, they say, but instead, it perpetuates trauma and jeopardizes the future of these children. Research shows that about half of Black children who go into care with the Child Welfare System in the United States and Canada will encounter the youth criminal justice system by the age of 17 years.

No solution is a magic wand that will fix everything. Multiple changes need to be enacted by deconstructing the current system. A Black youth said, "Our Black families can love and care for us, given the resources they need." Others have said that their families are hoping for a time when they will be treated by CAS according to their culture instead of being treated according to society's norms.

What is the meaning of culture? Example: A fish only discovers its need for water when it is no longer in it. Our own culture is like water to a fish. It sustains us. We live and breathe through it. What one culture may regard as essential – a certain level of material wealth, for example – may not be so vital to other cultures. (*Understanding Diversity by Fred L. Pincus, 2011*)

Black and minority youths who are involved in the Child Welfare System usually do not obtain support to form healthy relationships. I heard a mother say, "They took my child away from me, and now they want to send her back as a 'woman' because she is returning six months pregnant! This would not have happened in my home." Of course, she had no resources to support her teen as she lived in poverty, and that was the reason her daughter was taken into care. She was transferred to another foster home from the original intake home when she became pregnant. Luckily for this teen, her grandmother welcomed her into her home. The baby was adopted by a family who could not have any children.

Were you aware that Ontario's most vulnerable youths are being re-traumatized by a system that is supposed to protect them, and the youth justice system aligns with this system to set up the youths to fail? A research study carried out in 2018–2019 by Justice Brian Scully and Professor Judy Finlay, documented in the Toronto Star in January 2020, stated that the researchers were shocked to learn that the most vulnerable youths are shuttled from child protection to the justice system in Ontario. Foster and group homes have created the pipeline from the Child Welfare System due to poorly trained or untrained caregivers' inability to deal with traumatized youth. They fail to recognize defiant, disruptive, or aggressive behaviours as expressions of pain. When youths act out their trauma, the police are called to help de-escalate or intervene in the crisis. Instead of working with the personnel to de-escalate the situation, the youths were hauled off to jail when, at times, there was no danger to the staff or the youth.

The emphasis placed on the police for managing behaviours and subsequent instability is particularly catastrophic for Black and minority communities. It is seen as a culture of racism with the group care systems that allow these young people to be mistreated at higher rates than their non-racialized peers.

The Child Welfare System refuses to act as sureties when a Black youth becomes involved with the youth criminal justice system; some lawyers are insensitive to the struggles youth face in the child protection system and the unreasonable bail conditions that leave them languishing for months in pre-trial detention. Over the two years of the project (2018–2019), the researchers followed twenty-eight youths in care in Toronto who were involved in the justice system. During the two years, these youths spent 138 days in detention awaiting trial due to systemic barriers that make obtaining bail difficult and re-offending easy. Nine of the twenty-eight youths spent 1–6 months in pretrial detention, and eight spent more than 6 months. One of the Black youths spent 455 days served in two stints of detention, including one of 401 days! Of the twenty-eight Toronto youths, 57% were Black. That is higher than the overrepresentation seen at that time in the Children's Aid Society of Toronto data.

So, why is there a delay in obtaining bail? Is it because the Child Welfare System refuses to provide sureties, won't accept them back, or the bail conditions make their return impossible? If the police or the courts decide that a youth cannot have contact with another resident in the foster home, this requires a new placement, so as they take their time to find a new home, the youth lingers in jail. The youth may then be sent to another group home far away from their communities, where their cultures are not reflected. Black youths spent a longer time in pre-trial detention, an average of 200 days. The researchers called the children and teens they followed "cross-over youth"; they started in the Child Welfare System and crossed over to the Justice System.

CHAPTER 6

Policed & Punished

Quotes from "Black Youths Leaving Care"

Education is a gateway to opportunity and self-sufficiency. Finishing high school is a minimum requirement for most jobs. Completing at least one year of high school can boost a person's lifetime earnings. Youths who aged out of the Child Welfare System are sometimes not enrolled in school, and some barely complete post-secondary education. The designated age for exiting care is not correlated with a young person's abilities or readiness for independence. They are left to worry about living independently, finding decent, affordable housing, earning enough income, lacking financial literacy, and completing their education. They face such disadvantages, starting with a lack of community and family support, which makes it difficult to transition and puts them at risk of failure. Society sees these youths as dependent on social assistance because of unemployment or underemployment, leading to an intergenerational cycle of poverty.

> *Children in foster care have wings, but they need someone to teach them to fly, lead them in the right direction, and be there when they fall.*

> *CAS was my legal guardian for eight and a half years, and I feel as if they treated me like a burden and left me to fend for myself with no other help, like I was just a caseload, and my file is now closed.*
>
> *I feel like I am very limited; I don't even know how to use email… a deaf interpreter if I need to make a phone call or write to someone. I need to be more independent and take care of things on my own; for instance, if I go to a doctor, there is no interpreter. I can't even communicate, and it is very frustrating. I want to be able to, as a deaf person, have access to interpreters and be involved in the world.*
>
> *I didn't get to finish high school. I had to move schools several times, and I have always bumped around because of my moving status.*
>
> ***– Youth Leaving Care hearings,***
> ***Ontario Legislature, 2011***

Were they not removed from their parents' homes because of poverty? Some become homeless, which leads them to the youth shelter system, couch surfing, and staying in places that were not created as resting places. They are more likely to become involved with the Youth Justice Criminal System. What has society gained by placing these Black and minority youth into the care of the Child Welfare Services?

We must move beyond saving children to ensuring families have what they need to be healthy and safe. Our Black children and their families should be supported through wraparound care, which provides a comprehensive range of services that include the voices of families investing in their children's lives. This support encompasses resourced housing as permanent residence, mental wellness, job training, career development, and fostering emotional and social connections within their communities. Being caught up in the Child Welfare System has very adverse outcomes for Black and minority youths and their families.

The Complexity among Family Units

A family unit is defined by its members, and each family defines itself. A family can include people of various ages who are united through biology, marriage, or adoption, or who are so closely connected through friendships or shared experiences that they are considered family members. Family dynamics are constantly evolving, redefining their roles and relationships. The systems need to move beyond narrow, traditional understandings of who is a family for the youths they serve. How do families manage in communities when outsiders impose their definition on them, yet leave them to scramble for a living?

Highly educated foreign-trained professionals are seen working as security guards or taxi drivers because of the expensive, complex, and time-consuming process of becoming a member of a regulated profession, such as a Registered Nurse or Physician. These requirements leave some family members struggling to meet basic needs.

There are obstacles for new immigrant families to find suitable employment because of the requirement for "Canadian Experience." They question how they could gain experience if they are barred from any employment at the outset. The Public Policy forums describe the requirement for Canadian experience as a "retroactive condition" placed on newcomers, impossible to fulfill without first being part of the workforce. (*Erik Liu, 2007*)

Canadian experience is a euphemism for "You are not like us. We don't know if you can fit in with us, and we don't know if you work like us."

Single parents may be overrepresented in low-skilled jobs, working several jobs to survive, and having some of their children who are left unsupported and vulnerable. They live in poverty and, at times, in low-income community housing.

Divorced parents, where the youth's biological parents do not live together, need to provide ongoing family support. Without a father, the youths miss a male role model.

New immigrant and refugee families face challenges as they settle into and adjust to a new country's norms. Youths may arrive suffering from post-traumatic experiences, undiagnosed, along with mental illness. Perhaps a new mother or father is in the family unit, and the youth is missing past family and friends.

Some adolescents experience conflicts in their home settings. Instead of supporting the parents to develop skills to build relationships with their children, they are taken into care by the Child Welfare System. Many youths are re-traumatized, moving to different homes, and often feel they do not belong anywhere. When adolescents experience chronic exposure to traumatic events, they are more likely to develop complex trauma disorders. Their prognosis for healing and recovery is expected to be more negative. They will require comprehensive trauma-informed care provided by professionals.

Foster parents who act as parents at different points often focus on the negative behaviours reported during transfer. They usually do not see this as a crisis in the lives of the youth. They are not going into different homes because their behaviours have been good; they are sent to these other homes with negative labels demonstrating challenging behaviours that are very difficult to manage. These youths may have shared information with their teachers, noting that they are experiencing difficulties at home, and the Children's Aid social worker is called. I do not consider these situations to be high risk or neglect, which require reporting. Communicating with parents is crucial; the Children's Aid Society is called, and the parents are informed afterwards.

My Question: Why is the Child Welfare System not built for family preservation and reunification as opposed to traumatizing children? The fact that the human spirit can survive and thrive against all odds is truly remarkable. A few youths have overcome the trauma of being housed by CAS by utilizing tenacity and resilience, acquiring skills to leverage their strengths, and having a mentor. It takes one adult to mentor a youth into believing in himself and that he can reach his potential.

A Lived Experience

Norman, a 14-year-old new immigrant to Toronto, lived with his father and stepmother in an apartment building. After 6 months, he had made no friends and did not want to attend school. He asked his dad if he could return to the Caribbean island where he had previously lived with his grandmother. He said, “No, you came to live here with us, and that is what you will do.” They accompanied him to the family doctor on two different occasions over 6 months to have him assessed to get some answers to why Norman was seen as being “down” and disengaged from life.

The family doctor told the parents that he was just a lazy young man and needed to get out to school, meet other teens, and begin his life here in Canada. What was unknown to both the parents and the family doctor was that this youth was taking smaller doses of his psychotic medication so that it could last for a longer time. It was not known that he was suffering from a depressive mental health disorder, and he was very ashamed to share this information with anyone due to the stigma of having a mental illness.

Norman awoke at 12:30 a.m. one night and could not remember where he was. To him, it seemed like he was still living in the Caribbean, so he got up and went outside the apartment building. He wandered up and down the street. A police officer drove by in his cruiser and saw this young man wandering the street. He stopped and asked him what he was doing on the street late at night.

The frightened youth began to argue with the officer, saying, “Leave me alone, get away from me!” The police officer assumes the worst: a Black teen walking in the neighbourhood late at night, perhaps looking to rob or hurt someone. He called for backup from fellow officers. A fight ensued, and Norman was arrested and charged with assaulting two police officers. He was detained to await his court hearing the following morning, during which he might receive bail or be held in custody longer before a trial.

In detention, Norman fought with the youth service officers and was placed in a secure isolation cell, where he promptly fell asleep. At 6 a.m., he was awakened to go to court and would not come out of his cell or respond to any directives. He was agitated, tearful, restless, and appeared sad. It was decided that he would have a court appearance by video. He did not respond to any of the questions that the Justice of the Peace asked.

He was remanded in custody to have an assessment completed by a psychiatrist. When he was seen later that day, he was diagnosed with depressive disorder and provided the required medication. The psychiatrist also requested that Norman be placed in a healthcare observation cell to facilitate monitoring of his behaviour and to ensure he was safe. A plan of care was developed within the team of physicians, social workers, youth services officers, and nurses. He would be provided with a quiet environment and allowed to walk in the hallway when he became agitated in the locked cell. The officer would talk with him, offer refreshments, facilitate telephone calls with his parents, and inform the other team members of any specific needs they could not accommodate. This plan was developed during the day tour of duty, and the expectation was that all staff on all shifts assigned to Norman's care would facilitate his care as directed by the plan.

Not following the directives in the plan led to a very negative outcome for both the caring youth services officer and the detained youth.

John, a compassionate White youth services officer, worked the day tour of duty and was involved in developing Norman's care plan. The youth was walking in the hallway when this officer prepared his notes at 3 p.m. before going off duty. He shared this documentation with the officer who was replacing him. John explained what had occurred throughout the day and handed over the notes and care plan to his evening colleague. His colleague then observed that the youth was walking in the hallway and said to the youth harshly, "Get in the damn room; you are not allowed to be walking in this area. You need to be in the cell right now!"

John responded that Norman was allowed to walk in the hallway and that this was explained in the plan of care. Juno, his colleague, ignored this information, reached out, and pushed the youth down the hallway toward the cell. The youth became agitated and argumentative and refused to move. Juno asked John for help, but it was denied. Juno then called for backup officers and a manager to converge in the hallway. These youth service officers and the manager were not involved in the plan of care and did not inquire into the cause of the conflict. They fought with Norman, dragged him into the cell, and locked the door. John and the RN tried their best to explain the support Norman needed, but no one listened, and the attending manager reprimanded John in front of his colleagues.

John informed his manager about the occurrence, and the manager reprimanded him, stating, "We do not manage Black youths in this manner here. They are supposed to stay in their damn cells while waiting for a court appearance, whether he is mad or not!" John was so angry that he vowed to inform the senior administrator. He went to the administrator's office and was told that what happens in a department stays there; two managers had reported his behaviour, and this incident would be recorded in his file. He was in tears by then, so he went to the parking lot and sat in his car.

John went home, contacted the office of the most senior administrator, and was given an appointment to come to the downtown office. This individual needed to discuss the occurrence with the facility manager before meeting with John. When contacted, the manager became enraged that the incident had been discussed within the institution's hierarchy. Now, he was required to document the events and send this information to the head office.

John returned to work the following day as scheduled and was not assigned to Norman. He placed his lunch in the shared fridge in his work area. When he retrieved it at lunchtime, someone had disposed of the contents and replaced it with a rotten egg. He then went to the healthcare department and asked to speak with the on-duty psychiatrist. This request was granted as he seemed quite distressed. Note that the psychiatrist was at the facility to assess and treat the youth in custody, not the staff. He observed that John required immediate emotional support because he appeared very distressed. He was assessed and given a note for his manager to grant him sick leave that afternoon. He was also advised to visit his family doctor for further evaluation. His manager granted the request and told him that if he planned to be off duty the next day, he would need a note from his family doctor.

The situation worsened. He went to his car, and all four tires were slashed and flattened, and keying was found along each side of the vehicle. He called the police to report this, and a tow truck driver was also contacted to pull his car to his home. He became very ill from the traumatic events, depressed, despondent, discouraged, and unable to return to work. Gossip in the facility was that John deserved what happened because he was a whistle-blower.

Do you, as the reader, think that I would have been protected from a similar horrific outcome if I had gone to the highest level of the hierarchy to share information about the abuses I observed that the Black youth had been receiving? I guarantee that the situation would have been worse for a Black female healthcare leader.

Turning to the youth, Norman stayed at the custody facility for an additional day, and his mental health worsened, so he was transferred to a psychiatric unit at the local hospital. Due to his illness, which was diagnosed as chronic, when he was stable in the hospital, he was discharged to a diversion community support program, and he benefited from receiving support from his parents.

Back to the issue of John. He experienced severe retribution as a youth service officer who only wanted to help maintain an environment conducive to helping the youth's mental well-being. In his diversion from the code of silence, John's life was negatively affected. On top of this, other issues were added to the mix:

- There is a lack of training for some officers on how to support incarcerated youth.
- Transfer of correction officers from an adult custody facility to a youth custody facility when the adult facility closes.
- The union's contract bans a junior youth service officer from working full-time when doing so would affect the job security of a senior correction officer.

- **Job Insecurity:** A senior correction officer with years of experience could lose their job if a junior officer is kept on the job.

Thus, it is understandable to see conflict and strife across various workplace dynamics, as well as inner conflict among corrections officers, who lack job security and fight for it, recognition, and favours from their superiors. The youths and these correctional officers often clash because they are untrained to deal with troubled youth.

John, faced with retribution and broken mentally, physically, and psychologically, no longer works in the youth criminal justice system and had to begin a different career elsewhere.

Trauma Experienced by Black Youths in the System

Trauma is a threat to physical and emotional well-being. It is often reported as being overwhelming, having feelings of fear, lack of control, vulnerability, and helplessness. Teens who have suffered chronic trauma (such as being transferred to several different foster homes) have reported that trauma changes their view of themselves, the world, and others around them.

Young people experiencing trauma not just by being the direct target but by witnessing and observing violence in their communities or their homes are known as having vicarious trauma. Trauma can be difficult to discuss because the same event can be experienced by others and not be traumatic. In Black and minority youth, trauma can be a daily occurrence. An adolescent goes to school and, when classes are dismissed for the day, prepares to leave the classroom for home. While packing a knapsack, the alarm sounds, alerting all students to stay in the classroom and not look out the windows. The school is now on lockdown due to a serious crime that occurred on or near school property. This youth's activities are curtailed for several hours.

Not all young people will experience trauma in this situation. Still, for the Black youth who has already experienced trauma while living in a low-income environment, where violent crimes have occurred, this becomes a trigger, resulting in increased emotional and psychological stress. When a person has experienced the impact of trauma, though this may have been identified and treated by a professional, the memory of the traumatic situations may decrease, but the brain never forgets. Recurring trauma is not always in the immediate event, but in a similar previous event.

Some adolescents who have been traumatized may not access treatment due to several reasons. They may not understand the changes that have been occurring in themselves or find the words to inform others about such changes, such as anxiety, lack of self-confidence, insomnia, trouble focusing on school, and feeling ashamed of sharing these changes with friends and family. Some youths who have been through trauma do not want to talk about the situation that occurred. Still, if a loving, compassionate person takes the time to talk with the youths about observation, this could be the beginning of accepting and accessing help toward trauma-proofing.

A youth who has experienced trauma in the community and now enters the youth criminal justice system would become re-traumatized with the unequal and harsher treatment due to the way they are seen: Black skin, tough, gang-involved, suspended, or expelled from school, one-parent family where the parent is working two low-paying jobs and cannot be there to love and support the adolescent. Trauma does not go away without being professionally treated and making lifestyle changes, which is not possible during incarceration.

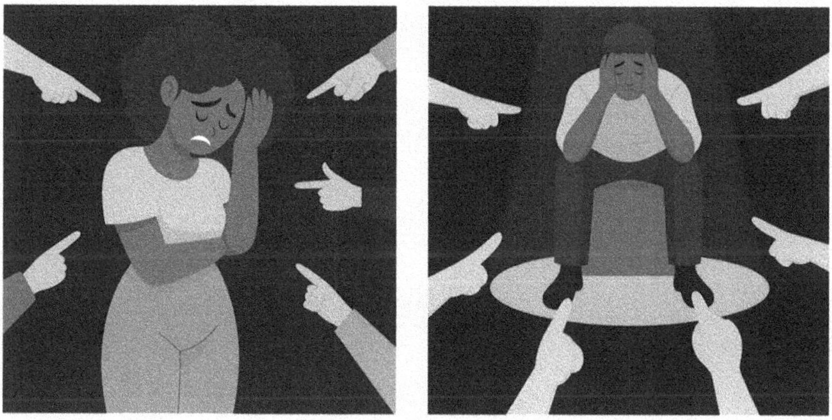

Teens are traumatized and asking for help, and folks around them think it is attention seeking.

Policing the Lives of Black Youth

Folks who read the newspapers and listen to various news sources will remember a significant event in Toronto, Ontario, on November 21, 2011. It is a perfect example of how Black youths can try to do everything right but still be arrested and charged for the "crime" of being Black and poor. (Being treated differently based on their race.) It was reported in the daily news that four Black teens – three aged 15 and the other 16 (two of them brothers) – were walking together. These youths were doing precisely what others of different nationalities would do. They all lived in Toronto Community Housing at 145 Neptune Drive. At about 6 p.m., they left their home and headed to the Pathway to Education neighbourhood mentorship program. They were stopped by police officers, who asked them to identify themselves. These officers were members of the now-defunct Toronto Anti-Violence Intervention Strategy (TAVIS).

One of the 15-year-olds had recently attended a program where he learned about his rights as a resident of Toronto. He asked why they were being asked to identify themselves near their homes. The officers told them they were enforcing the "Trespass to Property Act." Remember, this was their home; they were not trespassing. The 15-year-old, who knew his rights, did not readily comply. He was stripped, searched, and placed in jail overnight. The other youths were charged with assaulting police officers.

This case was held up in the criminal justice system for over a year, as these young persons were also identified as having previous contact with the justice system.

Fortunately, a security video surfaced to show the police encounter. The crown withdrew all charges. With a lawyer's assistance and community support, a report was filed with the Office of the Independent Police Review Director (OIPRD). While the entire incident lasted about a minute, the complaint process took 10 years to be resolved. By this time, most of these young people had become adults. It has recently been reported that one of these young men was jailed as an adult and committed suicide.

Low-income neighbourhoods are persistently a contested space in that they represent the intersection of low income and racialization in many cities. One phenomenon established is that policing strategies concentrate attention in low-income neighbourhoods. This type of neighbourhood-focused policing creates conditions of criminalization of Black youths and often manifests into police brutality, as well as the experience of micro-aggressions in public spaces. Youths have described going into a convenience store to purchase an item, only to have security officers follow them around, checking their every movement. They pay for the product and leave the store, but there are other times they go to another store where someone is not waiting to criminalize them. Some youths living in these community spaces have suffered more trauma than you or I can imagine in two, three, or fifteen lifetimes. To experience severe trauma and overcome it requires long-term support.

I have not met any parent who reported not loving their children. Some are skilled in demonstrating their love, building relationships, and helping their children reach their potential to take their places in society while giving back to help others. Some parents and guardians, especially those who are new immigrants to Canada, face many challenges in helping their children understand Canadian laws, such as the justice system and how to prevent their children from becoming involved in police encounters.

I have called Canada my home for over 50 years, and I cannot think of one week when the news has not reported negative police encounters with Black and minority youth. Many police forces across the United States and Canada are exploring ways to work with youths before they become involved in the youth justice system. Past treatment of Black and minority youths at the hands of some police officers has left gaping scars, profound carnage, and deep trauma in their lives and their families. Kids who live in neighbourhoods that are highly policed are the target of a significant number of stops and frisks, report high rates of fear, anxiety, depression, and hopelessness, get hypervigilant, are always on guard, and don't trust police officers and other authority adults, such as teachers.

Imagine sending your six-year-old Black daughter to school where the teacher knows there are behavioural challenges in having this child highly engaged in the classroom. When the child does misbehave, who is called, not the mother, but police officers, who place handcuffs on this child? A very distraught mother was summoned to the school where her child had now experienced not only physical harm to her being but also emotional trauma! She even has a police record at the age of six. In the future, she will be known for having had previous encounters with the police.

Much has been researched and documented about systemic racism, the use of force application, strip searches, racial profiling, and the racial disproportionality of Black and minority youths caught up in the justice system due to the actions of police officers.

It will take collaborative efforts within organizations and institutions to publicly acknowledge the reality of racial discrimination in the delivery of police services to the community and the specific impact on Blacks and other minorities before any solutions for change can be enacted. It will take hard and dedicated changes to eliminate discriminatory practices and build trust with racialized communities. I am a Black woman and a former member of the Peel Region Police Services Board. I can assure you that some very caring, passionate, and devoted police officers go on duty each day to serve and demonstrate professionalism. In every organization, "a few bad apples spoil the whole bunch."

Ahead are a few positive examples of how the Peel Region Police Service in Ontario serves its communities of youth and families.

Facilitate an eight-week, highly paid summer employment program, Youth In Policing Initiatives (YIPI). Youths between the ages of 15 and 18 from priority populations and those who reflect the cultural diversity of the Region of Peel are encouraged to participate. The partnership between the police and Sheridan College has created a safe environment for young people to pursue personal growth opportunities at a critical juncture in their transition from youth to young adulthood. These youths must attend high school within the region, reside there, and be legally allowed to work in Canada.

The application process opens in late January or early February each year for the summer intake of students. They are issued branded-name t-shirts and are expected to pay for their transportation. A part of the training for these youths involves classroom instruction covering many topics related to policing and community outreach, fitness components, and police drills to promote self-discipline, alertness, precision, pride, and the tools necessary for teamwork and success in the community.

Each year, the need for this program grows, and when you see these youths enter on the first day, they are eager and waiting with bated breath to learn new skills. There is a graduation on the last day of the program, and students are recognized for their participation. A few students can also apply for leadership roles in this dynamic program the following year. Others also apply to join the police services upon graduating from college or university.

In the Region of Peel police services, the leadership team and the board recognize that there are many Black and minority children, youth, and their families who live in the region and who require community support to help them reach their potential. They have now enhanced their partnership with Sheridan College, not only to deliver the YIPI but also to engage Black youths in implementing upstream, proactive, and preventive interventions, and to achieve greater representation of the community within the ranks.

In this region, the police services have signed a Memorandum of Understanding (MOU) with the Ontario Human Rights Commission, committing to develop and implement legally binding remedies to identify and address systemic racism in policing, promote transparency and accountability, and enhance other racialized and Indigenous communities' trust in policing through the Peel Region. (*Source: The Ontario Commission's work with Peel Region Police and Peel Police Services Board, 2022*)

Public trust in police forces in North America has reached a crisis level, prompting several forces to explore alternative strategies for managing the crisis. In Waco, Texas, United States, the focus is on recruiting female officers who are perceived as using less excessive force and making fewer discretionary and race-based stops. The public also sees them as more compassionate and honest.

A female police officer reports that she loves policing because she enjoys learning about people's stories and engaging with them to understand how their paths crossed and how to improve a bad day. She knows that no one gets up in the morning and says, "I am going to be a troublemaker today." Many North American police departments, including New York and Los Angeles, have signed on, alongside services in Saskatchewan, Alberta, and British Columbia, to increase the number of female officers in their departments by 30% in 2030.

One internal issue to be addressed is the presence of women in traditionally male sectors. A boys club culture has, for decades, been cited as the reason the profession has remained predominantly White, male, and heterosexual workforce. Research has found that mainly hiring White female police officers has little impact on our diverse Canadian culture. Despite having stronger female representatives for longer than in the United States, problems with racism and sexism persist.

The hiring of 30% female officers in police departments must also involve the hiring of women from diverse cultures. Also, the fact that some female officers do not stay working in policing for such reasons as encountering sexual harassment, no provision for working selected schedules, or having daycare for their young children must be looked at. Police departments must also consider ways to help women succeed in policing by implementing practical changes. Please help them seek promotions, even with families, and ensure they not only stay but also become department heads. (*The Toronto Star, Gillis, A female fix for policing? 2023*)

Increasing education is an excellent tool for all professionals, including police officers. The police divisions must acknowledge and address the systemic racism that exists within the youth criminal justice system. Implement policies and practices that eliminate racial bias at all levels, from policing to sentencing. Training should also be carried out on treating Black children as children; they are not small adults. It is essential to remember the legislation in the Youth Criminal Justice Act, which gives directives on the many positive initiatives that police can use to help adolescents who are struggling to find a different path away from incarceration.

CHAPTER 7

Inside the Walls

The Consequences of Incarceration of Black and Minority Youths

Despite a drop in the number of youths who are being incarcerated, the numbers remain far too large. Black youths and other youths of colour are incarcerated at far higher rates than their White peers. These disparities are driven by biased decision-making. Decades of research have clearly demonstrated that incarceration is not necessary in the vast majority of cases of adolescent lawbreaking.

> *Juvenile justice is probably the area that is most ripe for reform, in the nice liberal sense of the word, simply because there is no getting around the fact that a teenage brain is not an adult brain.*
>
> ***– Robert Sapolsky,***
> ***Professor of Biology, Stanford University***

Incarcerating young people leads to devastating long-term consequences; it lessens their likelihood of success, including poorer physical and mental health, disrupted education that hinders future work opportunities, and social integration into society. Many become repeat offenders because of how they are treated during their justice experiences, which causes lasting damage.

While in jail, young persons are exposed to more trauma, toxic stress, dehumanization, maltreatment, and in-depth punishment. Many become homeless, hopeless, and suicidal due to trauma, isolation, and abuse.

The Good, the Bad, and the Ugly

Youths of colour experience racially disparate treatment at every stage of the youth criminal justice system. The lasting harm caused by detention, incarceration, isolation, and trauma reminds us of the need to serve the youths in their communities. Black youths are more likely than their White peers to be arrested and referred to court, and, when incarcerated, are often placed in out-of-home custody facilities. The root cause of these disparities is a pattern of systemic disinvestment in communities of colour. Children and youths most in need of support, including those with mental health conditions, are disproportionally caught in the youth justice system. (*Office of the Juvenile Justice System and Delinquency Leadership Conference, December 2023*)

Despite the lower youth crime rates, many Black males and other minority youths are still being incarcerated for crimes that Whites are not. Youths of colour are disproportionately detained at higher rates than Whites, even when they engage in delinquent behaviour at similar rates as White youth. Locking up teens is very easy, but once they are caught up in the criminal justice system, this most often tarnishes their whole future.

Some youths arrested are released on bail and either dealt with in community programs or have a return-to-court date. Those who were detained for immigration purposes and those who were waiting to go to a trial were often quite depressed and angry as they sat in custody and waited for their turn in the courts. Some were as young as 12 and did not fully understand what they did wrong. They were not yet found guilty of anything. They were presumed innocent until proven guilty in a court of law and refused to actively participate in learning new activities.

A study recently showed that Black people in Canada's most populous province of Ontario spent a longer time behind bars awaiting trial than White people charged with many of the same categories of crimes (*CBC 2017*). This is at times because the Black person was unable to secure a surety, which forces them to remain in custody.

Another group of youths in custody was serving sentences imposed by the courts for the crimes for which they were found guilty. They had mandated programs in which they participated.

A few interesting occurrences while the youths were incarcerated:

1. The requirement of a healthcare team to assess all youths within 24 hours of admission ensured much easier access to a healthcare professional upon incarceration. At that time, a few may require psychiatric or medical follow-up. A youth who arrived at the custody facility late in the evening and who was taking methadone in the community may be experiencing withdrawal symptoms. The doctor on call would be contacted immediately to order a calming medication until the youths could have a medical assessment. The names of these youths were

placed on a medical list to receive healthcare assessments and treatments within 24 hours. Occasionally, the nursing staff contacts the on-call physician for medication orders to ensure the timely delivery of required medication before the physician goes off duty.

2. Various practitioners were employed on part-time or full-time contracts and had scheduled work hours throughout the week, as required, at the facility. There was a mental health nurse specialist, medical physicians, a dentist, a physiotherapist, an occupational therapist, an audiologist, a psychiatrist, a psychologist, a social worker, and an optometrist. Access to healthcare professionals was significantly easier than in the community, particularly due to long wait times and limited access to certain specialists.
3. While incarcerated, a certain number of youths learned the cause of their behaviours and corrected them through various support programs provided by professionals and arranged community involvement. For example, community groups entered the custody facility and provided programming in areas such as carpentry, self-development, and culinary skills.
4. The youths who were healthy attended school while being incarcerated and gained some education, but not enough to reach the academic level. Some sentences were short, and therefore, the youths were not there for the time it would have taken to complete even a school year.
5. Some youths were diagnosed with various chronic health issues for the first time in their lives, such as mental illness (in large numbers), decayed teeth, decreased

sight, decreased hearing, old wounds that had not healed effectively, partial blindness and deafness, learning disorders, addictions, and illiteracy. Provided with medical assessments, the youths found out some of the barriers they had in life, but parents also began to learn about those disabilities and gained an understanding of the root causes of their teens' behaviours.

6. A collaborative process was developed by the court mental health workers, parents, and the healthcare team for the youth who was being admitted directly from the courts and was known to present with a mental illness managed with medications; that information was shared. On admission to the custody facility, the youth would have timely access to medication. The physician would provide a telephone order for one to two doses to continue the medication until a medical doctor or psychiatrist saw the youth within the 24-hour window. Many assessment rooms were allocated in the healthcare department, where the youth was brought shortly after admission to complete an assessment and receive medications.
7. There was also a signed memorandum of agreement (MOU) with the hospital that, when an incarcerated youth was admitted with a mental health crisis, the youth would be accepted to a psychiatric unit and would be guarded by two youth service officers. The nurse leader from the custody facility was allowed to visit along with a parent. This collaboration helped the healthcare staff to learn about the psychiatric care needs of the youths for their return to the facility. This plan also helped determine

whether that level of care could be delivered at the institution, which assured the youths and their parents/ guardians.

8. Some youths had diagnoses such as Type One Diabetes and required daily blood sugar monitoring and insulin injections; they learned about their diagnosis, effectively tested their blood sugars, and gave their own injections of insulin for the first time since they were diagnosed. They felt proud that they could do this instead of relying on a parent's availability.
9. About one-third of all male youths who are incarcerated are found to have a mental illness that is undiagnosed, and which causes the negative behaviours they demonstrate in the community. Researchers believe that the combination of mental health disorders that youths bring into custody, coupled with the adverse effects of being institutionalized, places incarcerated youths at a higher risk of suicide. A psychiatrist or psychologist assesses them and receives an in-depth professional assessment, suicidal observation, and individual treatment for health. The mental health nurse specialist facilitated bi-weekly programs for youths who sought help to manage the symptoms of their mental illness. You could see marked changes in the behaviour of a youth who became aware of what he could do to maintain his health.

Aha Moments

There were experiences in youth custody that I titled as Aha Moments because of their uniqueness in an environment where there were more dehumanization and trauma than kindness.

Aha Moment #1

A scenario from a youth assessed by the optometrist, who was found to have marked decreased vision, was provided with glasses. What an excellent outcome for this youth! He even had the opportunity to choose the frame for his glasses!

Young man, I don't know what you have been seeing in your world, but my assessment of your eyes tells me that most of your life has been dark because you haven't seen the real world. We will get you prescription glasses so you can enjoy a better world. In four days, this youth's glasses arrived at the custody facility, and he was given them to fit his size and sight (*Dr. Brown, Optometrist*). The youth's response will be remembered: "Oh my God, the floor is beige, and the walls are brown; I saw only black before! I can see my world; no one will mess with me now. I thought I was in a darkened area where everything had the same dark colour."

John's world changed that day. After refusing to attend school since he was incarcerated, he was up first thing the next morning and got ready for school. Just being able to see his world gave this young man's life new meaning. He was recommended for early release and community support.

Aha Moment #2

> *In some situations, if one does not laugh, one may become sad and cry.*
>
> ***– Norma Fay Nicholson, Author (2025)***

All youths who are incarcerated are provided with healthcare education in addition to the curriculum delivered by the public school at the facility. Some are illiterate, and many are unable to learn due to the stressful situation they find themselves in. However, at least once or twice a week after school, the youths gathered in the multipurpose room on the pod, under the supervision of youth service officers, to discuss their health. The youths informed the nurses about the topics they wanted to participate in and learn.

When frontline healthcare staff are busy and cannot provide the planned education sessions, the healthcare leader volunteers to deliver the 1-hour sessions. This day's topic was about the transmission of sexual diseases (STDs), prevention, and, if infected, how to access healthcare in the community. As the discussion continued and questions were asked, one youth asked how he could check himself to find out if he had chlamydia. I responded that for each male youth, if there are no swollen testicles or pain when urinating, this sexually transmitted disease could go undetected in males for a very long time, and can be transmitted to female partners without the male knowing. One way of finding out where there are no immediate symptoms was for the youth to go to the bathroom and squeeze the tip of his penis. If there is cloudy or watery discharge, he should ask to see a doctor at the facility to have a chlamydia test performed to confirm the presence or absence of the disease.

All eighteen male youths requested permission to go to the bathroom to take this test! It took over 30 minutes to facilitate the requests for all male youths, as they were escorted to the bathroom in pairs. Four youths reported they saw drainage from their penises. I completed the referral form for them, while four others reported that they could not tell because they were too nervous; three were later diagnosed and treated. So not only are incarcerated youths found to have infectious diseases, but sadly, some are only learning what they can do to keep healthy while in jail.

Aha Moment #3

I answered the phone in my office, and the caller was the registered nurse delivering medications to the youths in cottage four before they started their breakfast. She sounded quite anxious and stated, "Please come to Cottage Four right away; all the youths are wearing facial infection prevention masks and do not want to remove them to receive their medications." She explained further that the youth services officers on duty informed the youths that many had been complaining about "runny nose and sore throat" and that wearing the masks would prevent the spread of a potential flu outbreak to all who resided in that cottage.

On my arrival at the cottage, I saw all the youths wearing blue facial masks and sitting at three dining tables. I had to stifle my laugh; what a sight to behold! Breakfast was on the tables, and the youths sat with masks on, looking at their meals. I asked the nurse to meet with me in the server, an area not far from where they sat. I asked the nurse what she would like to do to manage the situation. She said it was an opportunity for education and identifying who among them was coughing. She was unsure if hungry young men would listen. We discussed a shortened version of infection control practices when some youths were coughing in the same environment as others. We agreed that a more extended version would be required later that day to allow the youths to have questions prepared, as they would typically do for any educational needs.

I spoke to the four youth service officers on duty, along with their manager, and asked them for their assistance in identifying the youths who were coughing. I suggested that it might have been a good idea to have them wear masks, but it would not have been fair to those who were not coughing. They identified five of the thirty-two youths with a "cold." I briefly reviewed infection control practices with the five youths and requested that they dine together in another area away from others and that they not attend school that day. An appointment was made for a physician in the healthcare department to assess them. The five youths were reassessed the following day; they had no further coughs and did not develop fevers.

Regular routines continued at all meals, with the youths occupying the large dining room. I am writing this story, smiling broadly, and I wish we could take a picture of that scene. How on earth did the officers expect these young people to eat their meals while wearing masks?

A true Aha Moment!

Some Examples of the BAD Meted Out to Incarcerated Youths

> *Even if I could find an eraser for my mind, these events are seared in my mind for a lifetime.*
>
> ***– Norma Fay Nicholson, Author (2025)***

Warning: Note the sensitivity of these situations and the risk of vicarious trauma. Again, the author stresses that it is in the beholder's sight as they go through the lived experiences.

Some youths became increasingly traumatized by the brutal treatment they received at the hands of those who are supposed to be providing compassion, rehabilitation, and caring. The sheer brutality of those who should be providing support to help them recognize ways to change behaviours challenges the willful ignorance of those in power who cooperated with the abuse.

The caring youth services officers who dared to question the behaviour of some of their colleagues faced retribution beyond what the mind could conceive. It is a stark reminder of the preservation of systemic racism within our society, and even in jail. What was astounding was that Black and visible minority officers were among those who showed no compassion for the Black and minority youths.

These were demonstrated in the following situation: *Go to urinate when you do not need to, but go because you are forced.*

The officer awakened the youth at 12 midnight and said, "Last call for the bathroom tonight. Everyone will be given their turn to go. Wake up!"

The youth in room 20 was awakened for his turn, and he responded, "Leave me alone; I don't need to go."

The youth service officer said, "You get your ass to the door, and if I need to tell you one more time, you will be sorry about this disrespect."

The youth remained silent and quietly came to the door, where he was again told to go to the bathroom. Now he is distraught and angrily responded, "Why the hell do I have to be awakened to go to the bathroom when I don't need to go? And I am not a baby!"

Another officer was called to assist in teaching this youth a lesson in obedience. He refused to leave his cell. He was dragged out of room 20 by both officers, who called for backup help to watch over the other youth on the pod. This youth was dragged along the concrete hallway as he continued to refuse to stand or walk when instructed to do so. He was dragged by his arms while his behind straddled the outside concrete and stones for several yards to the secure isolation cell.

He was then thrown inside and told, "You will stay there until you learn respect." Though having terrible pain in his behind and legs along with some bleeding through his pants, he fell asleep until aroused by the nurse who made an early round at 6 a.m. to see all the youths who were placed in isolation overnight.

On assessment by the nurse, it was observed that the youth had new and old blood on his lower back, and his buttocks had open wounds. He refused to tell the nurse what happened overnight. The nurse called a colleague to help with the assessment, stating, "You would not believe this youth's condition and that he must go to the hospital, as we are not equipped to stitch open wounds. I want a second person to assist with the assessment and document my observations with a witness."

The findings were reported to the officers on duty in the isolation area. They were also informed that the on-call physician would be contacted to issue an order to send the youth to the hospital. The officers needed to inform their manager so that two of them could escort the youth in an ambulance. The nurses documented their assessments, and a copy of the health records accompanied the youth to the hospital. The youth service officer was responsible for documenting the events and discussing the occurrence with his manager.

To protect the youth's privacy, the healthcare law allows the physician in the hospital's emergency department to share information only with the youth's permission. The youth required surgery and a four-day stay in the hospital. Through the intervention of the hospital's psychiatrist, the youth shared his story about what occurred when he refused to go to the bathroom. Due to the trauma he suffered, he remained sombre, withdrawn, and reluctant to speak to others during the hospitalization. He was not returned to the facility upon his discharge from the hospital. The hierarchy arranged for him to be transferred to another youth facility due to his ongoing misbehaviours that could not be managed in this secure Youth Justice Facility.

Without being further involved in the healthcare of this youth, I can assure the reader that he was treated as a troublemaker, and the trauma he experienced was not addressed.

I requested permission to visit the youth in secure isolation before he was taken to the hospital, and I listened to his concerns about the horrific treatment he had been receiving. I apologized and supported his wish that his case would be heard in court soon. He said he needed help and would ask for that in court, as he is living a hellish life. I did not discuss my conversation with the youth service officers as they did not report to me. Due to past response from the administrator where a youth in isolation was traumatized, there would be nothing to gain by informing him about this situation.

I could not sleep that night as the trauma played over and over in my mind, and I also lost another great working colleague who was traumatized by this incident and resigned. I called the Member of Provincial Parliament from the Ministry of Children and Youth Services. I asked if she would consider an impromptu visit to the facility one day to see how badly the youths are treated, especially in secure isolation. She demanded that I tell her what was happening. I explained that I could not report incidents directly to the Minister. She said she would protect me; I responded that there is no such thing as protection for one of the very few Black leaders in the facility where anti-racism is practiced daily. She then retorted, "If you do not want to share what is happening, you are a part of the problem."

So, your question as a reader may be, why not report this disgusting, horrific, and terrible situation when you are told that you would be protected from the highest level of the custody facility? In another incident, you have read what happened to a White youth service officer when he went above his manager and the administrator to report a horrific situation that occurred when he was on duty one day. In these systemic, racist, and toxic institutions, you stay quiet or retain your well-being by leaving the job. One person cannot make changes while you are an employee. Racism can kill your spirits when your value is to help others, and it can also cause you to become mentally ill.

Luckily for Michael, his court case occurred two days after his discharge from the hospital. I was not privy to the discussion in the court. Still, his mother came to the facility to obtain a 24-hour supply of his medication (this is usually given to the family with the hope that they can see a doctor in the community to obtain a prescription within that timeframe) and his belongings. She told me that with the assistance of a psychiatrist, Michael was able to share some of the situations about his past and present life, and he was allowed to participate in a specialized trauma assistance and life-skills program in the community. He would be returned to the court for a review if he did not follow through.

As you are reading about the terrible treatment of Michael while he was incarcerated, what would you do in this situation, and in a system that was not built by Blacks for Blacks?

- Would you have punished him for refusing to go to the bathroom when he did not need to go?

- Was the punishment he received equal to the behaviour he demonstrated?
- Do you think he was traumatized by this incident?
- Do you believe the other youth who saw the beginning of this interaction would also have been vicariously traumatized?

A Note about Secure Isolation

Literature review and statistical data carried out through a systematic review of Ontario Youth Justice Facilities by the Provincial Advocate for Children (2014) showed that solitary confinement of youths is seen as clinically distressing as physical torture. It is due to the enclosed physical space, extended hours of confinement, lack of mental stimulation, limited physical activity, restricted access to fresh air, restricted human contact, and controlled bodily functions and hygiene.

When young persons are subjected to these types of confinement conditions and deprivation, most can be expected to report moderate to severe psychological symptoms after a period. This kind of security is also found to be very harmful to youths who are experiencing trauma and/or mental illness. Their symptoms may become intensified, such as anxiety, suicidal ideation, and depression.

Several youths have reported, "I had nothing to do but stare at the wall all day." This kind of isolation practice does not reduce misconduct, violence, or recidivism. Research has shown that this type of isolation results in lasting detrimental effects on the individuals who have experienced being isolated and is particularly harmful for those with pre-existing psychological illnesses. It has also been found to increase the rate of suicide more than five times higher than that of those who live in the community.

The American Academy of Child and Adolescent Psychiatry and the United Nations have both released formal positions opposing the use of solitary confinement for juveniles in secure custody facilities because of the serious negative consequences. The goal of incarcerating youths in these facilities should be to increase public safety by rehabilitating them so that they can become productive members of society. Solitary confinement and isolation practices undermine these goals and place a young person at risk of further harm. (*Psychiatric Report, Volume 29, Issue 2, March 1990*)

CHAPTER 8

The Hard Road Home

Return to the Community

Re-entry can be a very challenging time for the youths, especially if they have a mental health illness, an addiction, and no family home. These are the youths who "fall through the cracks" and are caught up in ongoing crime and revolving door incarceration.

The most important factors for successful re-entry into the community are healthy teenagers, employment, access to education, stable housing, life skills development, mentorship, and social networks. Very few of these were offered to the adolescents at the large, secure youth custody where I worked. Many lacked the skills to access finances, continuing their mental health and addiction treatment, and rebuilding their family units.

There were some planned predischarge meetings when the youth is being returned to the community from the custody setting to be monitored by probation, to live in a specialized home, or to be on house arrest. When the youth was discharged directly from the court back into the community due to an unknown case outcome, there was usually no discharge planning. Some teens were also sent from the court with a referral to a community diversion program, while others were released on bail to wait at home with restrictions until another court date.

A few youths who were discharged from the custodial facility had no home, were given bus tickets, wore the same clothing in which they were arrested a month or two earlier, and had no choice but to enter the shelter system in the community. Some restrictions imposed on those youths were that they could not return to the community in which a criminal act was committed, nor should they be in contact with any of their past victims.

Though there is a Youth Criminal Justice Act that directs youths away from custody except in extreme cases, there are still significant challenges being faced when youths are incarcerated and released to their communities. Here are some of these points:

1. Changes in our approach to youth justice administration have not remedied the over-representation of Black and minority youths in the system. Society continues to view them with high levels of suspicion and monitoring, especially on re-entry.
2. There is overlap with the Child Welfare system because the youth justice system is seen as effective and comparatively well-resourced. Young people can be directed into the justice system inappropriately. The criminal justice system is often used as a substitute for child protection, mental health issues, and social measures. Incidents that could be managed in the foster home in which a youth was placed, the police are often called for help, and into the justice system they are admitted.
3. There is nothing built into the system to continue offering services that support the growth of youths upon their

return to the community, or even when they age out of the Child Welfare System at a time when they are particularly vulnerable. Documentation has shown that when a youth who enters jail from the CAS, that youth is not returned to the same foster care home.

4. Community agencies that focus on helping Black youths are devoting some of their resources to grant writing and other functions to secure the funding needed to do their work. They often do this annually, and if the funding is not granted, the program ceases, leaving those youths without support to remain in their communities. Long-term sustainable funding is required in the community to deliver wrap-around support.
5. When philanthropic agencies or different levels of government provide grants, they are typically for a specific time and not multi-year funding; therefore, they cannot accurately measure the long-term impact of some programs.
6. There is a lack of culturally relevant programming and transitional housing for youths in some communities.
7. There are mostly anecdotal accounts of programming outcomes, with no evidence-based tools for measuring program success. The system's various actors have their success metrics, such as the number of arrests, diversion, and program enrollment.
8. Gangs and organized criminals view youths as targets for criminal recruitment because they view the system as relatively lenient for those under 18 years of age, placing additional pressure on vulnerable youths.

9. Some youths lack the support of family and friends to change their behaviours and need timely access to community programs.
10. Others have no money to purchase their medications and seek treatment from behavioural specialists. Their health deteriorates in the community.
11. While in custody, the management team would have used the facility's address to obtain a healthcare card for the youths, especially those who had to visit a community specialist or go to the hospital. In the community, a youth must apply and wait to receive this card before accessing healthcare. They must also strive to obtain identification, such as a Social Insurance Number (SIN), which can be very difficult when one has no known address.

– Young adults and how their needs are being served in Canada, 2020; The state of Black and Indigenous youth in Ontario, Laidlaw Foundation, 2023

A traumatized family.

CHAPTER 9

Rebuilding Trust, Healing Youths

Pathways to Change: Recommendations and Calls to Action

We have the power to foster change when we come together in the community, deliberating, deciding, and acting. Change can be tough when one advocates for changes to the justice system and challenges the negative assumptions about Black youths. Change begins in the mind, and we must all commit to elevating our voices and being advocates for long-term solutions.

> *It is easier to build strong children than to repair broken adults.*
>
> ***– Sam Moinet, Former Teacher and Founder of Student Breakthrough, 2021***

There are Black and minority youths who are resilient, and amazingly, they can bounce back and function well with ongoing community support. There are youths who have been incarcerated for committing violent crimes, and with support systems in place on their release, they mature into productive career adults. Help parents understand how the systems oppress them and their children, and what skills they need to develop to become effective advocates. Parents and supporting communities must be actively engaged to drive change.

The decline in the number of youths who are incarcerated now in Canada gives me hope that the use of incarceration to manage the criminal behaviours of youths can be obliterated from our society. An updated review of the evidence documented by the Sentencing Project (2022) shows that incarceration of young persons is an ineffective strategy for steering them away from delinquent behaviours and that high rates of incarceration do not improve public safety.

Research consistently shows that youths who are released from correctional confinement experience high rates of rearrest, new adjudications in youth court, and even convictions in adult courts. Studies that track youth outcomes into adulthood have found that an alarming share of young people incarcerated in youth custody facilities are later arrested and imprisoned as adults. This data compares the outcomes for incarcerated youths vs. the youths who come in conflict with the law and are allowed to participate in community diversion programs.

Do you know any Black youths who were suspended or expelled from school, received no support to change their behaviours, and ended up in the youth justice system? Being incarcerated reduces the likelihood that the youths will graduate from high school. The re-enrollment rates of youths returning home from custody facilities are low. Studies show that incarceration also decreases college enrollment and completion, which in turn lowers employment prospects in adulthood.

Our society must commit to supporting effective alternatives to incarcerating Black and minority youths. Reversing the ongoing over-reliance on detention requires significant system changes, comprehensive reforms, and a shift in society's understanding and active participation. As always, there will be resistance to meaningful and lasting change. It will necessitate the effective use of alternative programs for youths, especially for those who have committed serious offences. (*CHANGE is POSSIBLE; I Never Gave Up*: Eddie Ellis, Author and a former youth, 2023)

How do we go about making changes to ensure that any youth, and especially Black youth, who experience over-incarceration are directed away from this horrific system?

We must first work collectively on prevention and community-based treatment modules to keep youths within their families, and we must include young people's voices. No decisions are made about youths without them. They are the ones who experience the negative aspects of the system.

I am unable to find stats on how our Canadian youth justice system tracks and reports the results of alternatives to incarceration in terms of public safety and youth success. System staff should examine these results to ascertain any differences by race, ethnicity, and gender. Then, compare the results of alternative programs to those of detention facilities, adjusting for young people's offending history and their risk of reoffending, as measured by objective, validated risk instruments.

Many Black and minority youths, once detained and waiting to be tried in court, miss out on opportunities in their communities, like attending school or staying at home on house arrest. We should limit the use of pre-trial detention.

One Canadian statistic that is readily available is comparing Black vs. White youths who are detained; the Black youths stay in detention much longer before they are taken to their court trial. Some reasons given are that those who live in the Children's Aid Society do not obtain bail because they need to be transferred to a new guardian, access to legal representation is often quite challenging, and some of these Black youths live in poverty or are homeless. In Canada, we do detain youths who live in poverty and have mental illness.

The Youth Criminal Justice Act presents numerous opportunities for system changes, but it is often met with negative attitudes and misconceptions. Individuals in the community and youth justice personnel say this Act offers "freedom" to youths who get in trouble with the law, as they are not punished. Many individuals say that the youths receive a slap on the hand when they commit crimes and are therefore involved in crime sprees. The YCJA focuses on several areas to rehabilitate and keep youths in the community, but not everyone understands the Act or supports the rehabilitation and diversion efforts.

The media's reporting of exaggerated news, such as suggesting that they be given the names and addresses of these youths, implies that the public needs to know more about them and that they should not be granted bail. There is often no consideration that these are children whose background makes them vulnerable to crimes, and they must not be treated like adults. Through various therapeutic approaches, combined with family and community support, individuals can mature into responsible adults.

To unlock the future for these young people, various short-term approaches are now being used to address the root causes. These approaches need to be evaluated for their outcomes before being implemented permanently.

Parents and communities are responsible for ensuring they have access to services and support that promote their children's well-being. When they are unsure, they need not be ashamed to ask for directives.

Systems such as schools, healthcare, policing, and the Children's Aid Society must develop cross-system approaches. Change can be very difficult, as it exposes systems and challenges assumptions. How can Black students navigate their way through a career when there are low expectations for them, and large numbers are suspended or expelled from the classroom? They are often referred to as underachievers, are frequently streamed into areas where they do not excel, and have low graduation rates. These systemic barriers need to be removed from the classroom.

The barriers that youths face within the justice system are enormous. If they respond to the negative treatment received, such as being arrested in areas for crimes they did not commit, "since they look like another Black kid," or if they run away rather than dealing with unwarranted questions, they are seen as guilty and suspicious, when in fact they are terrified and traumatized. In adolescence, Black children act impulsively, respond emotionally, test the limits, wrestle with their identities, and worry about what others think. But at the same time, they are intensely curious, wildly creative, deeply loyal to their friends and families. They want the world to be a better place for themselves and everyone who looks like them.

All levels of government and agencies need to collaborate with youths, families, and their communities to listen and understand what needs to change so that society benefits from measured outcomes. One approach will not solve all challenges; find different and honest ways. We all need to shift our mindset and overcome the negativity we hold about the youth. A lot of the negative approaches are embedded in systems and have even become normalized. Once educated and understand the impact of their negative actions, we need to hold people accountable for their actions.

Break down barriers, unlock their futures, help them heal from their trauma, value them, and help them raise their voices. Look for their strengths, not their weaknesses. Some Black youths are directly or indirectly trying to tell us what is happening, and often, we do not listen.

The Youth Criminal Justice Act has shifted its focus from punishment to rehabilitation, recognizing the immaturity of young people and promoting community-based solutions. We all need to collaborate to address the broader societal factors like poverty, racism, alienation, and the negative impact of social media.

Conclusion

Uncaged

This book was born out of the trauma I experienced while working as a healthcare leader in a large, secure youth custody facility in Ontario, Canada. After 13 years post-retirement from the facility, I am now hearing about worsening conditions for youths and the many outstanding professionals leaving, which prompted me to share examples of my lived experiences of the harsh realities faced by Black and minority youths. I have also included suggestions in this book on preventing Black and minority youths from entering the youth criminal justice system. Numerous research studies have been conducted, yielding similar findings that demonstrate youths can succeed in their communities, provided they have the necessary resources to thrive. Their delinquent behaviours will not change when incarceration is focused on punishment and keeping youths away from the skills they need to grow into adulthood.

I recently had the opportunity to facilitate a round table discussion with a small group of incarcerated youths, many of whom are Black. A few professional organizations educate these youths to prepare them for reintegration into the community. Most education sessions are organized, approved, and held on Zoom. I humbly asked if I could be allowed the privilege to participate.

I saw only the faces of the facilitators, not the youth's faces. Videos were not allowed to be activated. Except for the decrease in the number of incarcerated youths due to restorative practices and diversion, youths in the justice system continue to experience very harsh treatment, brutality, demeaning disrespect, undervaluation, trauma, and humiliation. The stories they shared would *bring a man to his knees*.

Imagine for a moment, you are watching two teens who are incarcerated and are playing, and one says, "We must stop; I think I have injured my wrist."

That youth experienced pain and decided that the only thing he could do, as directed by the healthcare policy, was to complete a request form to see the nurse at the next visit. He took this written request to the senior individual at the custody facility. She took it from him, tore it into small pieces, and threw it in the garbage.

The youth said, "She did this right before me and told me to stop playing around; not only did my wrist continue to hurt, but I felt like nothing."

I could only think of Maya Angelou's quote, "Hope and fear cannot occupy the same space at the same time; invite one to stay." Only fear would reside in this youth.

I strongly suggest that we heed the compelling evidence that shows us that incarceration is a failed approach for teens because it does not reverse delinquent behaviours. Research coming out of the United States through the Sentencing Project informs us that 70% of incarcerated youths suffer from one or more forms of mental illness!

Community healthcare programs that provide rigorous, sustainable, long-term funding of mental health programs would change this trajectory. (The Sentencing Project, Richard Mendel, Senior Research Fellow: *Why Youth Incarceration Fails*, December 2022)

Many systemic barriers in healthcare increase the threshold for entry into the Youth Justice Criminal System. Long wait times to access care, the cost of certain services, the lack of professionals who are culturally sensitive to the needs of Black and minority youth, and the stigma associated with having a mental illness. Having a mental illness is seen as being weak; some families fear being judged for not recognizing this in their children, and may have inadvertently contributed to situations that occur in the homes.

It is okay not to be healthy all the time, but young people should be encouraged to be brave and share their concerns with professionals and family members when they are unwell to obtain the support they need. Most youths try to act normally by covering up that they are unwell by using illicit drugs or alcohol, which only takes them down the *rabbit hole of crime.*

The major systems that contribute to poor outcomes for youths are the schools, Child Welfare, policing, and society's refusal to see Black children as children. The youths must be brave enough to share their health information with professionals and family members to obtain the support they need.

Most people outside of the youth justice system only know what they see on TV, which includes sensationalized stories and their own fears. Youth custody is not only a nightmare, but also a trauma center. Any youth who enters the doors is likely to experience trauma.

Takeaways

By sharing my experiences, I hope to educate and inspire others to advocate for and act on systemic change, such as emphasizing diversion and restorative practices, developing community-based support systems, and increasing access to mental health and rehabilitative opportunities.

We all have a responsibility to advocate for change. Could you start by sharing my lived experiences in this book, connecting with your provincial and federal parliamentarians, advocating for change in various available forums, and volunteering to make a difference? Many not-for-profit organizations are led by Black leaders whose vision is to engage other Black role models to be change-makers. Will you support them in advocating for change within the systems?

Early intervention is the most cost-effective way to achieve excellent outcomes. What would it look like to disinvest most of the funds used to keep these youths in jail, and instead redirect them to active, culturally focused community programs that include the right stakeholders? If you believe in creating accessible opportunities and resources for Black youths to remain in their communities and strive to reach their potential, advocate for these system changes. Parents and guardians, please do not feel ashamed to ask for help. You are not expected to manage all the delinquent behaviour your children exhibit.

A True System Reform in Maryland, USA

In 2014, Maryland sent 1,500 young people to correctional facilities for a variety of crimes. That was 50% more than it enrolled in evidence-based community family therapy, which allowed young people who were involved with the juvenile system to remain at home and continue attending high school.

Based on the measured results, the Juvenile Reform Act was established in 2019 to research best practices for the treatment of juveniles involved in the criminal and juvenile justice systems and to make recommendations for integrating contributing risk factors in understanding why juveniles engage in crime.

Eight years later, Maryland sent only 260 youths to juvenile placement facilities (jails), an 83% decline, most for serious offences. Meanwhile, twice as many youths (465) participated in evidence-based family therapy programs while living at home, including a substantially larger share of youths adjudicated for serious offences – 33%, up from 20% in 2014.

The turnabout resulted from a fundamental analytic shift at the state's Department of Juvenile Services: "We really have drawn a line at the agency, that we do not want to have kids incarcerated unless there is a public safety need to do that." Recognizing that incarceration is costly and counterproductive for youths and their future, the changes were made incrementally as positive outcomes were seen.

In California, legislation was enacted in 2007 allowing state commitments only for youths found guilty of serious and violent felonies. Over the subsequent six years, the population confined in state correctional facilities declined 69% (from 2.115 to 659).

There are many smart folks north of the border. So, I ask: *Why can't we emulate these excellent practices?*

Youths of all cultures need opportunities to connect and engage. Why do you think that some are attracted to what the gangs offer them? They have no confidence, see themselves as hopeless, and are not encouraged even when they make mistakes. Please help them find their voices for their own betterment and for the betterment of our communities.

Answers to the Short Q&A

1. Listen, do not interrupt, ask how you can be of help, and decide approaches together.
2. Non-emotional discussion, it depends on the outcome for a specific follow-up.
3. Engage in a discussion about what she would like to see, and parents and child plan approaches.
4. Ask how you can help; there are many ways. Use your child's strengths.
5. Always strive to hear how your child feels and what help the child needs. When planning a meeting with the teacher or guidance counsellor at the school, try to focus on the current situation and the expected outcome.
6. Listen, it is best to direct to a lawyer or legal aid.
7. Need several discussions on the impact and how we can work together for a positive outcome.
8. It is good to have an excellent relationship with your parents or another trusting adult. You can share your observations on how this is impacting you, and together, we can decide on a follow-up.
9. No fuss, no disrespect, "May I please call my parents?"
10. There are many areas of prevention you want to explore, and this should start at home.

Acknowledgements

I randomly chose individuals and asked how they would manage the delinquent behaviours of Black and minority youths in our community. I explained that I was conducting a random survey to learn from them before writing a book to end youth incarceration. They took the time to respond, and I thanked them for their response, whether positive or negative. They were of all ages, cultures, and ethnicities, and gave me feedback on what they would like to see discussed in this book.

Parents and guardians have said that they wish they knew more about the resources that are available to assist their teens to be successful in their communities, where Black and minority families are seen through the eyes of racism in many of the institutions in our country.

Youths have asked for tips in managing "situations" in schools that negatively impact their learning. Many hope to acquire creative skills to become resourceful and facilitate community groups that empower one another. They want to be involved in making their voices heard.

Some of the parents and guardians support the elimination of incarceration of Black and minority youths and hope to learn various ways in which they can help with prevention. When youths get involved with the Youth Criminal Justice Services, they are equipped with the tools to help them. Community members would also like to read about some of the experiences of incarcerated youths to advocate for change.

Thanks also to folks who informed me that keeping Black and minority youths out of the system is impossible. I've been called, "Norma, you are a dreamer." Others voiced doubts, asking where the youths would go when they demonstrated such delinquent behaviours in the community. They must be locked away to keep our community safe.

I humbly replied, "We will do this together, involve many system changes, and take many risks." I also shared that everyone has the right to understand the law and to participate in legal processes that affect them. To accomplish this, they require knowledge, including where to find accurate information and reliable assistance.

Do you take daily risks? Of course, we all do. We get in our cars to go to work, ride our bicycles, or even go for a long walk. We are risk-takers!

About the Author

Norma Fay Nicholson, MA(Ed), BA, RN (Retired), is a dynamic healthcare leader and changemaker in empowering vulnerable youths and their families. She is the CEO and Founder of "Youth Empowerment Services."

A career nurse for 46 years, her last leadership role before retirement was collaborating with community members and other stakeholders to develop a unique wraparound healthcare support for incarcerated youth. Community members have hailed her dedication to family development as truly embodying the spirit of the community transformation within high levels of collaboration.

She is highly educated about the need for Black and minority families to understand the justice system and how to use preventive measures to stay and thrive in their communities. She also knows about the stigma of mental illness, the disparities in the Canadian community, and how racism impacts lives in very negative ways.

Shortly after retirement, she authored her first book, *Young Lives on the Line; You Can Make Difference*. The contents of this book have been used for preventative educational outreach to encourage support and change the lens through which we view the challenging behaviours of young children and youth, focusing on understanding the root causes. These are the factors that put youths on a path toward delinquency.

Norma has written five non-fiction books with an educational focus on championing racial justice and addressing racism, thereby strengthening the well-being of minorities. Her dynamic public speaking engagements are delivered in schools, libraries, community youth programs, conferences, workshops, podcasts, and after-school programs. She is an ardent volunteer in a variety of community outreach programs and has been recognized for her impact on the lives of youths and their families. She brings together diverse experts to reflect on the complexity of our Canadian Systems. Being grounded in lived experiences and leadership proves that proximity to struggle produces the clearest vision for change.

Contact the author at:

norma.nicholson.58

@normanicholson43

n.nicholson.a805@rogers.com

https://youthempowerments.com

https://ca.linkedin.com/in/norma-fay-nicholson-7471a24

Accomplishments & Recognitions

1. The King Charles 111, Coronation Medal, was awarded to the author by her Federal MP in honour of the Coronation of His Majesty King Charles 111, and in recognition of her extraordinary contribution and service to the community.
2. The Associated Youth Services of Peel recognized the author with the Lois Rice Lifetime Volunteer Award as a Youth Diversion Mentor.
3. Social Justice Champion, recognized by Dr. Nikki Clarke, TV Producer, for a variety of community educational engagements, such as podcasts on her show.
4. Rose Fortune Award by Black History Foundation of Ontario for a lifetime of helping others rise.
5. Dedication to Youth Development Award by Citizens for the Advancement of Community Development for unwavering commitment to empowering and supporting young people.
6. Youth In Policing Initiatives, Region of Peel and Toronto, is an annual summer recognition for volunteering, educating, and outreach to youth.
7. Ubuntu Legacy for Seniors Program, Mississauga: the author teaches about the intergenerational benefits of seniors and youths and facilitates a book club.
8. 100 Accomplished Black Canadian Women (ABC Women), Honouree making an impact across industries as a speaker, panellist, and moderator.
9. The Mayor and Council of the City of Mississauga bestowed on the author, "The Key to the City," one of the highest honours that the city grants to an individual in recognition and gratitude for their service to the public and common good.

Key to the City of Mississauga

King Charles 111 Coronation Medal

Membership

1. Black Criminology Network, England
2. Black Mental Health, Canada
3. Association of Treatment and Justice Professionals, Canada
4. Canada Black Chamber of Commerce
5. Mississauga Writers Group, Mississauga
6. The Writers Union of Canada
7. Amadeusz Not-for-profit, Toronto
8. Black Legal Action Group, Toronto
9. ADR Institute of Ontario
10. Urban Alliance on Race Relations, Toronto
11. Ontario Justice Education Network, Toronto
12. Mississauga Arts Council
13. Arts Council of Canada

Bibliography

Contenta, Sandro, Rankin, Jim, Toronto Star: *A shocking report details how Ontario's most vulnerable youth are shuttled from Child Protection to the Justice System.* January 2020.

Hardy, Kenneth V., Laszloffy, Tracey: *The Teens Who Hurt, Clinical Interventions, To Break The Cycle of Adolescent Violence.* The Guildwood Press, New York. 2005.

Laidlaw Foundation, Published Report: *The State of Black and Indigenous Youth in Ontario*. 2023.

Maynard, Robyn, Policing Black Lives: *State of Violence in Canada from Slavery to Present*. Fernwood Publishing Company, Nova Scotia, Canada. 2017.

Mendel, Richard, Senior Research Fellow, Sentencing Project: *Systems Reform to Reduce Youth Incarceration*. 2023.

Mendel, Richard, Senior Research Fellow, Youth Justice, Sentencing Project: *Why Youth Incarceration Fails: An Updated Review of the Evidence*. 2022.

Mental Health Commission of Canada, Children and Youth: *The Mental Health Strategy for Canada: A Youth Perspective*. 2017.

Rover, Josh, Director, Youth Justice, Sentencing Project Report: *Ethnic Disparities in Youth Incarceration*. 2021.

Skeen, Michelle, Skeen, Kelly: *just as you are: a teen's guide to self-acceptance & lasting self-esteem*. newharbingerpublications. www.newharbinger.com. 2018.

Turner Consulting Group, Research and Policy Briefs: *Dealing With Incidents of Racism in Ontario Public Schools*. Issue 2. 2019.

Ungar, Michael: *I Still Love You: Nice Things Troubled Kids Need from Their Parents*. Dundurn Press, Toronto. 2015.

Youth Research and Evaluation eXchange (YouthREX), School of Social Work, York University: *Student Mental Health Needs, Ontario*. 2019.

Glossary

Incarceration: Refers to being confined in a secure location to serve a sentence or to be detained for a specific period

Isolation: It is the practice of confining a youth to a single cell for a specified period, with no interaction with others

Living spaces: Cottages, cell blocks, and pods are the living spaces in the custody facility

Systemic: Means affecting many systems, such as Children's Aid and schools

Youth: Can mean one or more

www.ingramcontent.com/pod-product-compliance
Lightning Source LLC
Chambersburg PA
CBHW041259210926
51847CB00009B/79
9781964644677